Something Worth Living For

❖

Something Worth Living For

❖

Noel Davidson

AMBASSADOR

BELFAST   **GREENVILLE**
NORTHERN IRELAND   SOUTH CAROLINA

Something Worth Living For

First Published 1997
© Copyright 1997 Noel Davidson

ISBN 1   898787   45 X

AMBASSADOR PRODUCTIONS LTD,
Providence House
16 Hillview Avenue,
Belfast, BT5 6JR
Northern Ireland

Emerald House,
1 Chick Springs Road, Suite 206
Greenville,
South Carolina 29609
United States of America

Contents

❖

Foreword 7

Introduction 9

CHAPTER ONE   Retrolentalfibroplaisa 13

CHAPTER TWO   Blind Child in a Big World 17

CHAPTER THREE   All Change 22

CHAPTER FOUR   On the Wrong Track 27

CHAPTER FIVE   A Dead Loss 31

CHAPTER SIX   Lost and Found 34

CHAPTER SEVEN   New Faith, New Friends 38

CHAPTER EIGHT   Up and Down 43

CHAPTER NINE	Useful at Last	46
CHAPTER TEN	Going God's Way	50
CHAPTER ELEVEN	Capernwray Hall	54
CHAPTER TWELVE	Here am I, Send Me	59
CHAPTER THIRTEEN	Torch Trust	61
CHAPTER FOURTEEN	Inner Healing	64
CHAPTER FIFTEEN	From Disability to His Ability	68
CHAPTER SIXTEEN	The Priest Hill Story	71
CHAPTER SEVENTEEN	'Singing for My Lord'	74
CHAPTER EIGHTEEN	'Something Worth Living For'	77
CHAPTER NINETEEN	A Very Special Ministry	81
CHAPTER TWENTY	Richard	84
CHAPTER TWENTY-ONE	'When you Stand Praying, Forgive'	87
CHAPTER TWENTY-TWO	Do You not have a Blind Dog?	91
CHAPTER TWENTY-THREE	Into the Big Time	95
CHAPTER TWENTY-FOUR	Travelling On	99

Foreword

It has always been a tremendous thrill for me, throughout the years, to witness many people achieve in their lives, that which others would have deemed impossible.

One of those such people would have to be Sandy Clarke. Her determined efforts to conquer the disability of blindness have at times not only left me speechless, but left many others wondering, 'How does she do it?'

Unquestionably, her secret has been her commitment to her Lord and the strength of faith to know, 'He can take my disability and turn it into His ability'. How many times have I heard her say that?

Throughout the years I have had the great joy, not just of knowing Sandy, but also of sharing with her the love of singing for the Lord. Her singing at times has not only blessed me but challenged my own soul. What a great example she is to us who know her.

Only eternity will reveal the blessing that Sandy Clarke has been to so many as she tirelessly keeps to a hectic schedule of meetings far and near to sing and testify of God's goodness and grace to her, in spite of her own personal circumstances.

My prayer is that the Lord will use this book as an extension to Sandy's ministry and service for the Lord to reach those who might have eyes to see, yet still live in the blindness and darkness of sin. May God bless you as you read her remarkable story.

Rev. R. T. William McCrea

Introduction

❖

It is a beautiful Spring morning.

As I sit to write this, the window of my study overlooks a flowerbed. In it the mass of snowdrops, with their white inner-petals delicately fringed with green, are almost finished. They tremble in the slight breeze. Waving goodbye. The crocuses, deep yellow, purple and purple-and-white-striped, are standing erect, patiently waiting to open wide in response to the sun's warming rays. A cluster of pale lemon dwarf daffodils have just come into bloom. Dotted all through the bed are primrose and polyanthus plants bearing flowers of red, blue, yellow and white.

The whole scene is a feast for the eyes.

The eyes that is, that work. That can see.

Did you ever stop to wonder what life would be like for you if you couldn't see? Couldn't appreciate the soft green of the grass, the deep blue of the sky, or a mountainside clothed with purple heather?...

Sandy Clarke is like that. She can't see. And she has never seen a thing.

She was born blind.

As I have come to know her over the past year, Sandy has shared with me the sense of frustration, of rebellion, of uselessness, that she felt as she grew into teenage.

Why did she have to be different? Blind. Handicapped.

One of the few things that did provide her with some measure of consolation and satisfaction during those early mixed-up years, was her love of music. And her ability to sing.

From she was very young, she sang, as a sort of novelty item, in the Fiesta Ballroom, near her home in south Belfast. She treasured the few shillings collected for her in the whip-round. Her appearance fee!

As a teenager she sang with a group until she was thrown out of it for aggressive and uncooperative behaviour.

Life was empty. Fruitless. Pointless.

Eventually it became totally intolerable.

She decided to end it all...

Then something marvellous happened. Sandy trusted Christ as her Saviour.

Her salvation made a wonderful difference to her once-turbulent spirit. She was now possessed with an inner peace the like of which she had never known before. Her future prospects were sensationally improved, too. She was now bound for an eternal home in heaven.

Becoming a Christian didn't change her physical condition, however. She was still blind. And what do blind Christians do with themselves? What use could one of them be to God?

Whilst writing this book I have come to appreciate two things more fully. The first is the problems that face a blind person in a sighted world. Indeed, the problems facing disabled people in an able-bodied world. The reliving of Sandy's experiences will have made me, hopefully, a more considerate human being.

I have been made more acutely aware of something else, something more significant, as well. It is the mighty power of God to transform a life...

On Friday 28th February, my wife and I sat with two thousand two hundred and thirty three others in Belfast's Waterfront Hall at the first Gospel music event ever to be staged in that magnificent building. During the evening Sandy sang a solo verse. It was touching to hear the blind woman's clear voice sing out with such depth of feeling:-

"No more crying there, we are going to see the King,
No more crying there, we are going to see the King,
No more crying there, we are going to see the King,
Hallelujah. Hallelujah. We are going to see the King."

How did God make such a miraculous change in Sandy's purpose and direction in life?

From a rebellious teenager to a responsible representative for Torch Trust?

From a bitter sceptic to a submissive believer?

From the Fiesta Ballroom to the Waterfront Hall?

This book tells that story.

As far as Sandy is concerned there is still one mighty transformation to come.

At the moment she still can't see. And for as long as she lives on this earth she won't be able to see. But that is all set to change too.

She is going to see one day..

And what's more, she is going to see the King!

The One who has loved her, saved her, and guided her through a life spent in His service, will one day receive her into His promised home in heaven.

To see Himself.

I trust that you are ready to join Sandy, as she in turn joins millions more, as we all meet together, on that day, sometime in the future.

To see the King.

May God really bless this book to you.

Noel I. Davidson.
March, 1997.

CHAPTER ONE

Retrolentalfibroplaisa

---- ❖ ----

The big day had come at last!

The day that Sandy Clarke had looked forward to so much for so long.

She had imagined it would be great. It would at least be something different. Surely it would be exciting too!

Sandy was just over five years old.

And today she was going to school. For the very first time.

Her brother, who was two-and-a-half years older, seemed to come home every day with yet another spellbinding tale of adventure from school.

What a fabulous place it must be!

It caused the eagerly expectant little one just a fleeting concern,then,when her mum explained to her patiently,on the long-awaited morning, that she wouldn't be going to the same school as Ronald.

Why that? She wondered.

Why not? She pondered.

Would her school be just as exciting as big brother's?

Would she too be able to recount tales of interest from the classroom and tales of heroism from the playground?

"I have to leave Ronald off at his school first," Mrs. Clarke told her very excited,but somewhat apprehensive daughter. "Then we will go on to your school. The one that you will be going to is a bit farther away ,so you can sit in your push-chair if you want to."

So little Sandy, for she was small for her age,climbed into her push-chair in the hall of the family home in the Donegall Road area of Belfast.

And waited.

She sucked her dummy hard.

Mother had been trying to wean her off it for months. "For going to school you know!"

But it was a great comfort at a time like this.

Having left Ronald off at his school, Sandy's mother pushed that buggy through the early morning bustle in the streets of south Belfast with a sense of purpose.

This was a big day for Sandy.

And for her as well. In a different way.

Meeting them were groups of chattering mothers and children. There didn't seem to be many going in the same direction as Sandy and her mum.

At least they hadn't caught up on any. That in itself was strange, for the buggy was fairly bombing along. Certainly nobody had passed them!

Funny. Peculiar.

On arrival at her school, Sandy was taken to a classroom and allocated a seat.   Her place was at a large wooden desk which was easily two sizes too big for her. The seat was small and hinged and hard.

Sandy's chubby little legs didn't even touch the floor. She half-sat and half-hung,suspended by her elbows, from the shining, sloping desk-lid.

It was her mum's conversation with the teacher, though, that brought it home to Sandy. Helped her to realize that her school was indeed going to be different from that of her brother.

"I will come back for her at two o'clock on Friday afternoon," she had promised whoever-it-was.

Friday afternoon!

Was she going to be away from home all day and all week? Every week?

Was this a sort of a day-and-night school?

The simple answer, as Sandy Clarke, aged five, was soon about to discover,was, Yes.

It was a day-and-night school.

It was a boarding school.

She was soon to understand also why the greater percentage of mums and their kids had been going in the opposite direction to her mum with her kid.

Sandy Clarke had been a premature baby and had been given too much oxygen at birth. This caused a very serious condition which the doctors had tried valiantly, but vainly, to rectify.

Retrolentalfibroplaisa, they had called it.

Everybody else used a simpler word to describe her condition. They just called it blindness.

It was only when she went to school, however, that she realized that most of the other children around her neighbourhood didn't live in her colourless domain.

In Ronald's school the pupils read thin books, using their eyes.

In Sandy's school the pupils read bulky books, using their fingers.

The five-year-old pupils in Ronald's school went home every afternoon at two o'clock.

The five-year-old pupils in Sandy's school didn't go home during the week at all. They stayed. Home time was Friday afternoon.

Sandy's first school was the Ulster School for the Deaf and Blind on Belfast's Lisburn Road.

All the blind pupils lived in. For very practical reasons.

As well as being taught how to read, in Braille, and count,the young blind children had to be taught how to perform simple tasks. Like how to dress themselves,how to manage at the table,how to cross the road.........

It was learning to cope.

Education for life, for real.

The boarding pupils were accommodated in large, impersonal dormitories. Even their nightwear wasn't their own.

Sandy Clarke's early school days were not the happiest days of her life.

There were many sleepless nights. And many tears.

But the school performed its function.

She learnt a lot.

She needed to learn a lot.

Blind children have a lot to learn.

CHAPTER TWO

Blind Child in a Big World

❖

Sandy loved to sing, and to listen to music.

When she was just three years of age her supreme delight was to sit on her uncle's knee and be bumped up and down gently, like a rubber dinghy in a slight swell, as he sang,

"Christ is the Saviour of sinners,
Christ is the Saviour for me,
Long I was chained in sin's darkness,
Now by His grace I am free."

She laughed heartily, too, when the volume of the voice increased and the slight swell suddenly changed to a moderate, or even rough, sea, for the chorus.......

"Saviour of sinners,
Saviour of sinners like me,
Shedding His blood for my ransom,
This is the Saviour for me."

Young Sandy hadn't a clue what the words meant. Not a notion.

But she liked her uncle, she liked the tune, and she liked the closeness and the comfort of the gentle rocking.

Moments like that were wonderful. Highlights. Treasured memories.

For growing up proved to be a rather painful experience for the little blind girl.   People made allowances for her. Welcomed her into their homes. Some, unwittingly, and with the best of intentions, went over the top a bit with their attention.

Treated her as some kind of a freak.

Establishing herself, then, as a normal seven year old, or eight year old, or nine year old,whose only problem happened to be that she couldn't see,turned out to be an uphill struggle.

Her skill on her trike, up and down the back entry, gained her some measure of acceptance. The speed at which she could zoom up and down, avoiding the bins and all sorts of miscellaneous junk, was a wonder unto many.

But those who accepted her for who she was, were by and large those who were older than her.

Her peers teased her frequently. And mercilessly.

"Go on, Sandy,tell me how many fingers I have up. Bet you can't!" they taunted.

It was cruel.

One of her proudest moments as a child was at a prize-distribution night in Donegall Road Gospel Hall. Sandy had been a regular attender at the Children's Meeting there, along with swarms of other children from the surrounding streets.The meeting on a Tuesday night had been a peak of the week for many of them throughout the long, dark, winter months.

Prize - night was the big climax. The grand finale.

Sandy was dressed in her best.

And so were the most of the rest.

Everyone sat agog,waiting for his or her name to be called.

"We have a special prize for Sandy Clarke," Mr. John Watson announced to the spellbound audience. "It is this big book." And he held up a substantial volume.

All eyes were by now rivetted on the "big book." Everybody waited in a curious, respectful silence as Sandy made her way, proudly but carefully, up to the front.

"It is John's Gospel in Braille, Sandy. We hope you will like it and read it," Mr. Watson continued, when Sandy had arrived up beside him.

The little eight year old girl's face was a picture.

She glowed with pride and blushed with embarrassment all at once. Others could see it. Sandy could feel it.

When the "big book" had been placed in her hands, she muttered a self-conscious "Thank you" to the kindly Mr. Watson, and returned to her seat.

Then the wonder commenced.

After the meeting was over and the bustle to get home began, Sandy didn't move. She remained in her place. Engrossed. Mesmerised.

Her fingers glided skilfully over the pages of her great treasure. Dozens of "normal" children, who had been presented with "normal" Bibles, crowded around to look.

They could see. Sandy could only touch.

"How could that pattern of bumps on a page make sense to anybody?" they asked each other in amazement.

When she began to realize that her "big book" had become a centre of attraction, a cause for commotion,Sandy became aware of an audience.

Audience or no audience, though, she didn't care.

She had been presented with something very,very precious.

A book in her own language.

Her very first, very own, Braille book!

When she was nine years old Sandy continued to develop her interest in music. And singing.

It was a different kind of music this time, however.

Two teenage girls who lived across the street from her in Broadway Parade, used to go to the Fiesta Ballroom. There they heard the dance music. And bought the records. The old 78's.

Sandy loved to go over to their home, for they would switch on the pick-up record-player for her and allow her to listen to the hit songs of the day. Big treat!

It didn't take the dead-keen youngster long to learn the words. Or the tunes. She was singing along in no time!

Then her friends had a bright idea. They would help their little chum!

One night they smuggled Sandy into the ballroom, and then managed to persuade the organisers to allow her to sing at an interval.

It worked!

Soon the blind nine year old girl became something of a novelty attraction.

She sang the pop-songs of the time to fascinated audiences,who,in turn, to express their appreciation, had a whip-round to "help the wee blind girl at boarding-school." Then she was whisked off home again, a few shillings richer, by one of her teenage "promoters", and the dance went on as usual.

Sandy enjoyed it, too, when the hobby-horse man came into her street.

"Roll up! Roll up! A penny a ride!" he would call at the top of his husky voice.

And roll up they did. Scores of them, clutching their big brown pennies.

But here again, Sandy was special.

She got free rides. The hobby-horse man would set her onto a riderless mount and she would glide round and round, up and down, sweetly soothed by the gentle motion and the jangling music.

Sandy used to spend whole summer days just going from street to street with him. Then when tea-time came she made her way home, rather reluctantly. Tired,dusty and content.

Every Sunday, come what may, the Clarke family went to granda and granny Carson for lunch. Sandy thought the world of them. They were such lovely people. Gentle, caring Christians.

She also loved to get round to their house for another reason. An ulterior motive, perhaps.

Granda and granny had a big wooden wireless!

So when her grandparents were out at church, and Sandy was in the care of an aunt who was happy when she was happy, she used to sneak into the parlour at noon and switch on Two Way Family Favourites.

How she looked forward to that programme!

And how she enjoyed it.

What wonderful, wonderful music! she thought.

She had to make sure that the big wooden monster was switched off, silenced, before the church-goers arrived home, however. Granda Carson allowed the wireless to remain in his house on one simple condition. It was never to be switched on on a Sunday. NEVER NEVER.

He was a Lord's Day Observance man, through and through.

On a few occasions he caught her on. In the dressed-up-and-waiting-time,the after-church-and-before-lunch-time, he popped into the parlour to chat to his little granddaughter. He found her sitting comfortably,and humming softly one of the tunes which she had just heard, but was certain sure that he wouldn't know.

" Sandy, you have been listening to that worldly music again!" he announced gruffly, and with apparent displeasure.

"What do you mean, granda?" Sandy protested innocently.

"What do I mean?! What do I mean?! The valves in the wireless are warm, girl! THAT'S what I mean!" he retorted.

Sandy wasn't scared.

Although she couldn't see the twinkle in his eye, she could sense the twinkle in his voice.

He had forgiven her already, she knew.

CHAPTER THREE

All Change

❖

When she was eleven years old, two very different but both very significant changes took place in Sandy's becoming-comfortable, established routine.

Either one of these changes would have been quite enough for any child to have coped with at a time.

But both, coming as they did, together, totally upset the status quo for Sandy. Mixed her up completely.

Both were moves.

First to come was a change of school.

Initially, Sandy was pleased when she was told that she would be transferring to a new school at Jordanstown. For two reasons. It was a beautiful, modern, purpose-built educational establishment. It would be a big change from the Lisburn Road. Secondly, and more importantly,she didn't have to board. She could go home in the evenings. Sleep in her own bed . Eat the things she liked. Talk to the family. The second major disruption for the young blind girl was a change of home. A flit.

The family moved house, across to East Belfast.

From a street house to a semi-detached with a bathroom and back garden would be anybody's dream.

Anybody, that is, except Sandy.

She didn't like it at all. In fact, she detested it.

Everybody who had tried to sell the idea of the new house to her had told her that it would, "be great to have your own back garden."

"Just imagine! Your own private place to play!" they had enthused.

So when the removal men had left,on that hot June afternoon,and her parents were red in the face,bathed in sweat,and up to their waists in tea-chests,cardboard boxes, and crumpled newspaper,Sandy decided to make herself scarce. Get off-side. Outside.

She would launch herself headlong into a new adventure.......

She would experience for herself that fantastic phenomenon.......

The back garden.

Two things impressed Sandy immediately as she stepped out of the back door on that sunny afternoon..And as the summer progressed, and the "back garden" experience became less of a novelty,those impressions proved to be lasting.

No matter what time of the day,or night, she went out at, still she sensed the same two things.

Always there, never changing.

The strange smells. And the scary,creepy silence.

It seemed that the familiar, fume-laden clamour of the Donegall Road must be at least a million miles away!

When her mum and dad were out with her in the garden they raved about it. "Oh isn't this just marvellous?!" they drooled. "How silent! How peaceful!"   Marvellous, maybe.

Peaceful, probably.

But silent certainly! Sandy heartily agreed with them there!

How she missed the constant chatter and banter of the neighbours as they rushed, or merely dandered, about in the street. How she longed to hear the clang of the bell on the door of Sally's little sweet shop.

And to hear Sally herself.

"Ach, and there's my wee Sandy!" she used to call in her broad Belfast accent.

"How are you theday, love?"

So Sandy became unsettled. Pining for Broadway Parade.

The fresh smell of newly-mown grass and the heavy summer scent of the roses in the back garden were pleasant, true enough. But they weren't even in the same League of Smells as bubbling tar that you poked with a stick, Bobby Grattan's chip shop, or the exhaust fumes from a passing No. 27 bus!

As Sandy advanced into teenage something happened that disturbed her emotionally.

Her older brother Ronald and her younger sister Marlene began to establish their own identity. Make and meet their own friends. Go out in the evenings and at weekends.

Ronald called it, "messing about with my friends."

Marlene, who was so much younger, described it as, "going out to play."

Then, as time and maturation both advanced, teenage romances sprang up and they seemed to jabber on incessantly about "boyfriends" and "girlfriends".

These developments were perfectly normal and natural. Part and parcel of growing up.

But Sandy didn't like them. They affected her.

Companionship and support seemed to be melting away.

She began to feel left out of it. Isolated.

Consequently, for the first time in her life, she started to feel really lonely.

Loneliness led to bitterness.

And bitterness bred resentment. Particularly towards her sister.

"Why do I have to be blind?" Sandy fumed to herself often.

"And why is it that SHE can see everything and everybody, go out and in when she likes, and bore us all to death talking about her hundreds of friends?

As for me.... Well what about me?

I can see nothing or nobody. I very seldom go out, so that means I don't need to come in, and most of the friends I have are in a school for the blind, miles away.

Why did this have to happen to me anyway, in the first place?

And there's another thing... Why is it, with all the clever doctors that there are supposed to be about, can nobody do anything for me?"

In her more rational moments Sandy had to give them credit for trying. For try they certainly did.

However, all that the specialists could do for her condition was to remove her right eye and replace it with an artificial one. This action had to be taken because of fluid pressure at the back of the eye.

A medically expedient, but definitely not an emotionally inspiring, experience. Not only was this mood of rebellion affecting her home life. It soon began to spill over into school as well.

The desk became a drum. Sandy just sat and hammered it for all she was fit most of the time, but she didn't use it for anything else. Lessons and learning were non-starters. Her only interest was in pop music.

The school staff and her parents consulted on the matter and came to the conclusion that it would be better for Sandy to return as a boarder. She would then at least be close to any friends she had.

Perhaps "settle her down a bit," they thought.

But being a boarder back in Jordanstown didn't make a lot of difference, really.

Sandy was now approaching adolescence, and discovering that music, and life, had a lot to offer.

Her teachers recognised her passion for music. And began to develop it. Some of the other teenagers who were with her at school shared her interest. Especially some of the boarders.

They were encouraged to set up their own musical group, and were highly praised for their performances at school concerts. A big date for the group was the occasional night out at the Carrickfergus Y.M.C.A.!

This involvement in the musical group thrilled Sandy and her friends. Proved to be very important to them. For some of them, including Sandy, it was like a lifeline thrown from the land into a stormy sea, just as they were going down for the final time.

It allowed them to recognise something vital.

That their world, though totally colourless, wasn't totally hopeless.

Around that time, when Sandy was in her early teens, a television talent show was very popular. "Tea-time With Tommy", it was called.

A family friend entered Sandy for it.

After a few months of nervous suspense the fourteen year old was invited to appear on the show,and she did very well. Made a big impression.

To her great delight, shortly afterwards, Sandy was promised an audience with Bridie Gallagher's manager.

This was marvellous! This was the big time!

What a boost for the morale!

Here was something which she could do that Ronald and Marlene couldn't.

She could sing.

Sing so well as to be noticed.

And to be noticed was important.

Imperative.

CHAPTER FOUR

On the Wrong Track

❖

The overwhelming desire to be noticed, recognised, acknowledged, provoked in Sandy the desire to do outrageous things.

In school she started a "gang", whose unwritten code of practice seemed to be, "If the school authorities say, "You have to do it," then we will show them that we don't. And won't."

It was total non co-operation. Rebellion. Defiance.

The music classes,in which the teacher endeavoured to introduce the students to the delights of some classical pieces, invariably ended up in rock-and-roll sessions.

As the school year progressed it came to the stage where Sandy was more often outside classes than in them. Turfed out for disobedience or insolence.

She derived a great deal of satisfaction from this . It was having the desired effect. She was establishing an identity. Building up an image. Being noticed.

Unfortunately for Sandy, however, the teaching staff realized what she was up to. Twigged on to her little game.

After some consideration they meted out measured and effective punishment. Hit her where it hurt.

She wasn't allowed to sing in the group anymore. Or go with them on their outings to the Y.M.C.A.

Now the lifeline had been withdrawn. Pulled back to the shore, for the drowning girl hadn't seemed to be using it.

But Sandy was still wallowing in a sea of despondency. Howling gales of hopelessness whipped the waves into a frenzy.

She sank deeper and deeper and deeper into depression.

Her mother took her to the doctor, who talked to them for what seemed ages, and then gave Sandy tablets to take.

Tablets to take. Now here was a new idea for her to muse upon.

Tablets to take. What would happen if she took more of them than she was supposed to? Exceeded the stated dose?

She thought it over for a while. In classes, and out in the corridor. In the dining room and in the dormitory.

Eventually she came to the conclusion that she had nothing to lose. She could only win.

If she took an overdose, and it took her life, that would be the star prize. The jackpot. She would then be finished with physical affliction and mental misery. Great.

On the other hand, even if it didn't kill her, but only knocked her out for an hour or two, she would still be guaranteed a bit of attention. And that would at least be something.

So one day Sandy put her plan into action.

She took an overdose of her tablets.

However, fortunately for herself, Sandy couldn't resist the temptation to broadcast her intentions in advance. Brag about it to all and sundry.

"I am going to take an overdose of my tablets some day," she had told her mates often, but they didn't take her too seriously.

"Don't talk nonsense, Sandy," they used to reply. "Surely you can't be that daft!"

Their comments only served to strengthen her resolve. "I will. I will do it some day, you'll see," she had assured them.

When Sandy turned ghastly pale that evening, and then became violently sick, a partially-sighted lad who had heard her suicide forecasts realised what had happened, and rushed for help.

Her plan had misfired. She had to accept the consolation prize. Psychiatric help.

These sessions helped a little, but still the seeds of discontent and the roots of rebellion sprouted below the surface.

Then, one Friday afternoon, something happened which brought to an end Sandy's schooling at Jordanstown. .

In order to help prepare them for the big-wide, largely-sighted, world of work, the school was developing a policy of encouraging independence amongst its teenage pupils.

One of the methods used, amongst others, to help advance this policy,was to expect the senior pupils to make their own way home at the weekend.

This meant that they had to get to the proper station or bus-stop, buy tickets, board the bus or train, dismount at the correct stop or station, and then make it on home after that if a parent or friend wasn't waiting with a car.

Easy enough when you can see! Not so easy when you can't!

Nonetheless it was sensible stuff. Preparation for life, for real, again.

On that fateful afternoon, Sandy and her friend Betty set out on this challenge for the very first time. They were reasonably confident that they could do it. If others had done it before them, surely they could manage it too.

Each bought her ticket successfully at Jordanstown railway station.

On stepping out onto the platform they heard, but ignored, the whispers, "There's two of them blind girls from the school over there."

Just one problem, however.

It hadn't crossed anyone's mind to tell the two blind girls that the platform, at that point, was only about four metres wide.

So Sandy and Betty strode boldly forth across it. Arms linked. Confident.

Then all of a sudden what a shock!

Both of them stepped together off the edge of the platform. Into thin air.

They ended up in a tangled mass of humanity on the railway track below. And the train was expected at any moment!

Frightened yells rent the air. They both screeched simultaneously.

The standers-around suddenly sprang into action! The whispering soon stopped when the rescue started!

Eager hands pulled the two terrified teenagers to safety, just before the train came hissing in. It was three minutes late. What a mercy!

Betty and Sandy were bruised, cut and extremely shocked. The train had to be slightly delayed while the porters escorted them into a carriage and made sure they were comfortable.

On arrival at York Road station in Belfast, Betty went home with her parents, and Sandy with hers.

However, when they reached the house and Sandy complained of a very sore shoulder and a terrible pain in her head, her parents decided that it would be best to take her across to the Royal Victoria Hospital for a check-up. "Just in case."

Following an initial examination, the doctors told Sandy's parents that they were keeping her in overnight for observation, as she had symptoms of concussion.

During this stay in hospital, other medical complications became evident. These, in turn, meant that Sandy needed much more treatment than had ever been anticipated when she was admitted on the day of the frightening fall.

Thus with the summer term well advanced, and Sandy Clarke not well at all,the holidays came around and she was still off.

And that was her finished.

She never returned as a pupil to Jordanstown School

CHAPTER FIVE

A Dead Loss

❖

When the doctors were treating Sandy's medical condition they discovered that she had other, potentially more serious, problems.

Psychiatric ones.

It was at this time, after careful consideration and a number of interviews with her parents, that the consultants in the hospital decided that Sandy should be admitted to a psychiatric unit called Windsor House. This unit was attached to Belfast City Hospital and specialised in the treatment of adolescents with emotional and psychological problems.

What a mixture of young people were there!

Some were ordinary youngsters.

Others knew what it was to get into, and be in, trouble.

Some were of school age. Others were older.

Classes were held in the unit and the students were all expected to attend for three hours every morning. Since the aim of the unit was to promote independence in its young people, there was no school in the afternoon but the residents were encouraged to go shopping and mingle in the community.

Whilst they didn't do a lot of shopping, the young people certainly mingled in the community with great relish!

Sandy loved it!

Cafes with juke-boxes and slot machines became favourite haunts. Some of the senior chaps in the unit had powerful motorbikes and they gave the girls pillion-rides. For Sandy, roaring down the Lisburn Road on the back of a 750 c.c. Norton, with her hair streaming out in the wind, was a world far removed from the restrictions of Jordanstown. There could be no comparison.

It was a real dream. Imagine, being allowed for the first time in her teenage, to mix with ordinary, lively, sighted youngsters and "live it up" in the big world.

But it is in the nature of dreams to come to an end. And often abruptly, causing the dreamer to wake up with a start. Bewildered. Disorientated. Upset.

This was Sandy's experience.

The first trauma that she had to cope with was another operation.

Pressure and fluid had built up behind her remaining natural eye, the left one, causing her a lot of pain. Doctors were left with no alternative but to remove this eye also, leaving Sandy with two artificial, sightless eyes.

She became increasingly bitter and rebellious.

Why did all these things, one after another, have to happen to her?

And to crown it all, what had been Sandy's dream, the freedom of Windsor House, had been her mother's nightmare. When she realized how her daughter was "just wasting her time", she campaigned tirelessly to have her transferred to somewhere else.

The authorities understood Mrs. Clarke's anxieties, and granted her request. Sandy was accorded a place at a rehabilitation centre for blind teenagers in Reigate, Surrey, England.

This move was to prove a disaster from the start.

Sandy arrived at the centre, only to find that others had beaten her to it , and arrived first. These others were people from her former schools, and who knew her past.

They teased her relentlessly.

They bullied her ruthlessly.

Sandy couldn't stick it. She just couldn't cope.

She became terribly depressed. Life, for her, was totally, utterly, unendingly black. Unmitigated gloom.

The only way out of this tunnel of misery, she reckoned, was to end it all for good.

So she tried to commit suicide, for a second time.

And this time she almost succeeded.

When she was discovered in her bedroom, with an empty tablet bottle beside her, Sandy was unconscious. She was rushed to hospital and resuscitated.

From that there was no going back to the rehabilitation centre.

Sandy was shipped home to Northern Ireland, in disgrace.

She was a failure. And she knew it.

"A dead loss", was how she described herself, to herself.

Sure she couldn't even manage to commit suicide right!

CHAPTER SIX

Lost and Found

❖

No school.
No work.
No centre.
No friends.
No fun.
It was boring.

Sandy Clarke was depressed, sad, lonely, unsettled and insecure. Various types of tranquilisers were prescribed for her but they did nothing to lift the depression or brighten the gloom.

She spent whole days in bed, listening to the radio or the record player. Her mother tried, in vain, to persuade her to get up. What was the point? What was there to get up for?

Very occasionally she was asked to sing at a concert or function.

This was great while it lasted. Music. Company. Acclaim.

But when the next morning came and everyone else was back at work, or if it was a Saturday, out with their friends, Sandy just stayed in bed. And she was still in bed in the afternoon.

What was the point in getting up? There was nothing left to get up for.

It was at this time of unrelieved despair that a friendly couple came into the blind girl's life.

They invited her to a Gospel meeting.

Now Sandy was no stranger to Gospel meetings. Or the Gospel message.

Her aunts and uncles had told her often about the love of God, and she had been to many meetings with them.

She accepted the kind couple's invitation, not because she had any burning desire to go to a Gospel meeting, but because the prospect of going "up to the house afterwards for supper", seemed too good to miss.

Up at the house, after the meeting, the lady and her husband talked to Sandy, and listened sympathetically as she poured out her problems.

The blindness. The bitterness. The loneliness. The emptiness.

"God still loves you, Sandy. He loved you so much that He sent His son, Jesus, into the world to die for you. And He's not going to stop loving you now," the husband explained, graciously. "No matter how useless, or sinful, or bitter, or resentful you feel, God still loves you. And He is calling you to come to Him for salvation. For peace, and rest, and satisfaction."

None of this was new to Sandy. She had heard it all before. Many a time.

Although she had heard the message so frequently, and had often been challenged by it, she had always held back from making any commitment to Christ.

There was something about the prospect of salvation that worried her. She had a secret fear.

In the warm and homely atmosphere of an after-supper-chat with a caring Christian couple, she voiced her nagging concern.

"I would like to be saved, but I know that I could never keep it!" she blurted out, emphatically.

There was a short silence. Precious thinking time.

"You know, Sandy, Jesus is the Good Shepherd. When He goes out and finds a lost sheep, He never, never lets it go. And it's the

Shepherd who keeps His sheep. The sheep don't keep Him," her host continued, his tone of voice gentle and encouraging.

By the time she reached home, later on that evening, Sandy's mind was in turmoil. Snippets of conversation, verses from the Bible, and lines from choruses all raced around in it, pell-mell. She kept turning them over. Again, and again, and again.

Nobody on earth seemed to be able to do anything for her. That was for sure.But could God?

She rolled into bed. And rolled over and over in the bed. Sleep was far away. As she lay there, thinking, suddenly her roller-coaster mind ground to a halt. Her thoughts began to focus on two verses which she had learnt, many years before, in Sunday School. They were from Isaiah chapter 53.

These verses stayed with her.

Sandy began to repeat them to herself...............

"But he was wounded for our transgressions, he was bruised for our iniquities: the chastisement of our peace was upon him; and with his stripes we are healed.

All we like sheep have gone astray ; we have turned every one to his own way ; and the Lord hath laid on him the iniquity of us all."

As she pondered those verses, in the hushed silence of the middle of the night, Sandy realized that they described her so well.

She was one of those lost sheep.......

She had certainly gone astray....

She had wanted to do her own thing.... Establish her own identity.... Make a name for herself....

But did God really love her?

Could He really do anything for her?

Blind, rebellious, depressed Sandy Clarke. Could she possibly have this wonderful joy and peace and satisfaction that the Christians kept talking about?

Deeply moved, she slipped out of bed and fell to her knees in prayer.

"God, if You are there........ If you really exist.....Please, please do something for me," she pleaded, earnestly. "I'm one of your sheep, and I have gone astray. Thank you, Lord, for dying for me. Forgive my sins, and just take me. I will do my best to trust You, and to serve You. Amen."

No spectacular signs accompanied that heartfelt commitment.

No brilliant light rent the darkness of her bedroom.

No mighty earthquake shook the house to its foundations.

No booming voice thundered in her ear.

But Sandy knew that deep down in her heart something momentous had happened. As she knelt there that night, the 20th April,1970, she was saved.

By simply coming to Christ as she did, Sandy had been accepted by Him.

She had done important business with God.

CHAPTER SEVEN

New Faith, New Friends

❖

Sandy Clarke had met with Christ. No doubt about it.

The next morning came. How did she feel?

She knew that inside, something had changed. Something was different. In her heart there was a sense of calm which she had never known before. The turbulent, rebellious spirit had come to rest. She had found peace, at last.

Having just experienced something wonderful, Sandy wanted to tell somebody all about it.

But who would she tell? Who would be interested? Would anybody care?

How would her family and friends react to her news?

She began her public witness to her newly found faith by telling her parents.

Their response was, "That's good, Sandy."

"That's good", and that was all. Full stop. No more. They didn't appear to be too bothered, either way.

Sandy thought that her granny would be pleased when she heard. And she was right on that one. Granny was thrilled. Called Sandy's conversion, "an answer to prayer". That,at least, was encouraging.

Then she told the lady who had invited her to the meeting, and who had, with her husband, been instrumental in leading her to Christ.

Sandy had expected her to be overjoyed. And show it.

Throw her arms around her, or jump up and down. Do something memorable.

Maybe shout, "Hallelujah!" a time or two.

So she was just slightly disappointed, then, at her friend's somewhat muted reaction.

The lady was pleased, and said so, but she was also a little cautious.

Delighted, perhaps, but certainly not demonstrative.

She assured Sandy that she would help her in any way she could, and that she would be remembering her in prayer.

As she spoke to more and more people about her simple commitment to Christ, Sandy grew more and more determined to prove to them that it was real. She would show them that something exciting had happened in her life. They would see that a tremendous change had taken place.

But what could she do? How could she prove anything to anybody?

She had been a blind, failed, nineteen-year-old dropout from everything.

Now she was merely a saved, blind,failed,nineteen-year-old dropout from everything.

Did that one word, that single experience, make any difference?

There were three things that Sandy wanted to do. All three were desires that had been born in her soul as she knelt by her bedside that April night.

She wanted to worship God. In sincerity and in truth.

She wanted to know more about the Bible. For although she had kept, and in a way, treasured, her "big book", her John's Gospel in Braille, she had never ever read it. Reading the Bible hadn't been part of her "image". Now she just wanted to read it, and read it, and read it and learn all she could about its message.

And she wanted to meet other Christian young people. There must be dozens of them around out there, and wherever they were, Sandy wanted to find them.

But where, or how, would she begin, to attempt to achieve her threefold ambition?

Sandy's granny would gladly have taken her by-now-Christian grandchild to her church, but Sandy wasn't particularly keen to go there. She was under the impression that her granny's church was specifically a granny's church. There were not many young people in it, or much life about it, she felt. It would be far too straight-laced for her. Too much of a culture shock.

Where could she go, then? What should she do?

Friends encouraged her to try different services in different churches. When she did, she found that she really liked some of them. There were young people in those churches, Christian young people like herself. She had no problem with the churches.

So it came as a shock to her, when she came to the sickening realization, after a number of months, that the church leaders had a problem with her.

Not that they didn't like her. For they did.

Not that they didn't believe that she was a Christian. For they did.

Their difficulty was a very practical one.

How do you cope with a blind young woman? Would it be wise to take her on the annual outing to the seaside, for instance? Who would take responsibility for her?

And what about the weekend camp? Definitely too risky?

Sandy became aware of, and in a measure understood, their dilemma.

She could sense the air of restlessness. Hear the nervous whispering.

This, in turn, made her feel uneasy. Guilty, almost.

She felt let down, too. And blamed her blindness.

Here it was, this blindness thing, this barrier, getting in the way again. Spoiling things for her. It always seemed to be spoiling things for her.

Why, oh why, did she have to be born blind?

She decided, then, that she wouldn't allow the problem of her blindness to be a problem for the churches any more. And the solution was simple. She just wouldn't go.

For a while she didn't.

This led to further isolation. And frustration. Spiritual mixed-up-ness.

Unknown to her, though, God had His eye on His sightless child.

Help and solace came in the person of another woman.

This kind Christian lady was Irene, wife of the evangelist, Hedley Murphy.

Irene was a tremendous support to Sandy, through an extremely difficult period. She plied the young, struggling convert with a steady, but not overwhelming, stream of her husband's Bible teaching tapes, and Gospel records.

These proved to be a real life-line.

Stepping-stones across a rushing, raging torrent of uncertainty that threatened to sweep her off her feet, and carry her out to drown in the sea of oblivion.

Guiding-stars of hope in a night of black discouragement, where she had just begun to wander about aimlessly.

After a number of months of this supported, house-bound, spiritual solitude, two Christian girls whom Sandy knew invited her to attend an evening coffee bar, organised by a Church which she had never been to before, Glengormley Baptist.

Sandy was pleased to go. There might even be company, young people of around her own age, there.

When seated at a table, she was surrounded by happy and helpful teenagers.

They appeared warm and welcoming, normal and natural. What thrilled Sandy more than anything else, though, was the fact that they treated her as a long-lost friend, and not as a one-off freak.

During the lively, question-and-answer, getting-to-know-you conversation, her tablemates discovered that Sandy loved music, and could sing.

They encouraged her.

"Would you like to give us a song now, Sandy?" they enquired. Inviting, but not pushing.

Sandy was delighted to be asked. But what would she, what could she, sing? Most of the songs that she knew well enough to sing upon impulse invitation were the pop songs of her early teen-age. Hardly appropriate for this occasion!

For someone wanting to sing Christian pieces, blindness posed another practical problem. At that time, not much material had been produced in Braille. So all the verses that you wanted to sing, you needed to know off by heart.

And Sandy didn't know many. Yet.

Having given it a moment or two's thought, she realized that there was one piece which she had listened to so often on one of the Irene-lent records, that she knew every single word of it.

So when Sandy burst forth into song, it was what she sang.

A hush descended on the bustling coffee bar, as her voice rang out............

> "Just a closer walk with Thee,
> Grant it Jesus, this my plea,
> Daily walking close to Thee,
> Let it be, dear Lord, let it be............"

Everyone seemed to appreciate it.

One of the girls turned to Sandy, after she had sat down again, and asked, quite pointedly, "What church do you go to?"

Silence reigned again. Only over one table this time, though. Although she couldn't see them, Sandy could sense the gaze of half-a-dozen interested young people. They were awaiting her reply.

With bowed head she whispered, ashamedly, "None."

Her new friend's response was immediate.

"You will never be able to say that again!" she replied, enthusiastically. "You can rest assured that you will be at one on Sunday morning. And every Sunday from now on, for that matter. We will pick you up."

And they did.

Sandy Clarke's happy association with Glengormley Baptist Church had begun.

CHAPTER EIGHT

Up and Down

❖

Sandy was happy now. At last. Happier than she had been for many, many years.

She loved Glengormley Baptist Church.. She had made new friends. Genuine friends. Christian friends. In the Pastor's daughter, Joy, Sandy found someone who shared her by-now-restored fun-loving approach to life, but who also coped with physical disability.

Joy suffered from a serious heart condition, so she and Sandy were a bit slower than most of the other young people. They had to be more careful, for different, but obvious reasons.

The two friends worked out a practical scheme, which was repeated Sunday by Sunday, for companionship on the way to Church. Sandy walked to the end of the road where she met Joy. Then they made, and took, their own time in walking along to Church. They enjoyed many happy, leisurely and spiritually refreshing Sundays together. Each of them so much appreciated the company of the other. And all the other young people also accepted them for who they were.

Sandy loved it all. She felt so complete.

Through church contacts, at that time also, she became involved with an interdenominational group called The Young Life Campaign. This movement arranged a lot of missions amongst young people and Sandy took an active part in the work.

Her participation in such varied and valuable activities gave Sandy a tremendous psychological boost, as well as providing a focus for her Christian life.

But changes were about to take place, yet again.

Although things seemed to have taken a turn for the better for Sandy, both socially and spiritually, yet there was still no possibility of employment. Trying every means they could arrange to help her, Social Services decided that she should attend a rehabilitation centre for adults with disabilities, this time in Torquay.

When Sandy first heard of it she was upset.

She didn't want to go.

Why did she have to leave the church, Joy, Young Life, and all her new friends?

"To train," was the answer she was always given to her oft-asked question. Had she been a normal nineteen year old she could have enquired about a job at the Labour Exchange, or looked for one amongst the dozens that were advertised in the Belfast Telegraph. But then, she wasn't a normal nineteen year old, so she had "to train".

"Blind people need special training to equip them for employment," she was reminded repeatedly.

This blindness was still an obstacle. Always spoiling things.

Her friends in the church encouraged her to undertake the course, assuring her of their support.

So Sandy went to Torquay.

Not only had her church encouraged her to go, but they had also taken steps to prepare the way for her. They had contacted a lively and caring Baptist Church in the town. The folks in that church were very kind to Sandy. Did everything they possibly could to make her feel at home.

And it worked. She felt at home with them.

In Torquay, Sandy experienced first-hand and for the first time, something that has become very precious to her with the passing years. It was that there is a genuine warmth of Christian love amongst genuine Christian people wherever you go.

Unfortunately, she didn't feel just so much at home at the rehabilitation centre.

Sandy's condition, which had been caused by too much oxygen, had also brought with it another problem. A side effect.

Her brain to hand co-ordination had been impaired.

She tried really hard.

Not like Jordanstown. Where she had tried very little.

Not like Windsor House. Where she hadn't tried at all.

She tried really hard.

But her hands just refused to do what her brain told them to.

Craft work was obviously not for her. Mats and baskets were not within the bounds of her physical capacity.

And she had so much wanted to succeed.

For God. Who had altered the whole course of her life, and had given her the desire to do something worthwhile for Him.

For her friends. Who had placed so much confidence in her.

And for herself. For more reasons than she could count.

But they sent her home. With nothing.

Empty-handed. Empty-hearted.

What would the church think?

What would the leaders of Young Life think?

Worst of all, what did God think?

She felt a total failure, a walking disaster.

Deep depression returned.

CHAPTER NINE

Useful at Last

❖

Life back at home was even more lonely. Especially during the day. All Sandy's friends from Glengormley Baptist Church were either in employment or away at college.

What was she to do now? Where did she go from here?

Employment for the blind had classed her as a failure. Given her up as a hopeless case. They weren't going to be of much help.

The visiting social worker helped as much as she could. But she couldn't find Sandy a job.

In her loneliness and frustration, Sandy began to realize that she had available to her a powerful resource which she hadn't used in previous crises.

Prayer.

She poured out her heart to God in prayer, confessing her sense of uselessness, explaining her desire for usefulness.....

Repeatedly. Fervently. Desperately, almost.

And God heard, and answered her prayer.

Although she had thought that she was all alone in her misery, and that everyone else was too busy to be bothered, Sandy discovered that she had been mistaken.

Some of her friends, who understood how she felt, had been very concerned about her. Had been praying, and planning, for her.

One of these caring people introduced Sandy to Finlay Packaging, a printing and box-making firm. Although they had a full-time telephonist, it had been considered necessary to engage an additional temporary member of staff to help out on the switchboard during a particularly busy period.

So Sandy Clarke was employed, for the first time in her life. She was thrilled, but found, when she commenced in her new job, that there was so much to learn.

The lady who operated the switchboard was partially sighted, so she could, to at least some degree, appreciate Sandy's problems. She proved to be incredibly kind and patient as she trained the new recruit. In addition to working as a telephonist, Sandy also performed other menial tasks around the office. Like sealing envelopes and sticking on the postage stamps.

By many standards it wouldn't have been considered as either a wildly exciting or extremely rewarding job.

But for Sandy it was fantastic. Something to rise for every morning. A reason for living. An answer to prayer.

She wasn't in it for the money, although she liked the sense of independence that a few pounds of her own afforded her. She was in it because she felt that she was doing something useful, no matter how small or insignificant her contribution would appear to be.

At last she felt important. Used. Wanted. She was somebody, doing something. Not just a nobody, doing nothing. Best of all, too, even her disability was accepted. The other girls in the office treated her as an equal. Not as some sort of an odd-bod for whom special allowances had to be made.

After the initial training period, and when she recognised the recent employee's increasing capability as a telephonist, her supervisor began to undertake other clerical duties, leaving Sandy in sole charge of the switchboard. Marvellous for the self-esteem!

The period of steady employment permitted Sanndy to steady herself. It restored her self-confidence. This in turn allowed her to become more and more involved in Christian service.

She began to participate actively in outreach work with Glengormley Baptist Church and the Young Life Campaign. She was afforded great opportunities to witness for Christ.

People began to want to hear her. She had so much to tell. God had been so good. Her faith continued to grow and blossom.

After a few months of this constant activity, Sandy had climbed out of the valley of depression and was gently ascending the hill of self-assurance. The sun of acceptance shining on her back warmed her through and through. It was pleasant.

As she started to travel around her immediate area, kindly transported by Christians-with-cars, Sandy met many new Christian friends. In many different denominations. And discovered that there were many different interpretations of the teachings in the Bible.

Occasionally she worked with some people who believed strongly in the ministry of healing.

They assured Sandy that she could be cured of her blindness. Made to see. Like everybody else. The barrier broken down. The obstacle removed. It sounded almost too good to be true, but her friends firmly maintained that it was possible.

Since they all appeared so confident, Sandy agreed to allow them to pray for her. That her sight would be restored.

One memorable Friday night she was taken around to someone's house, where a number of sincere Christians had gathered, to pray for her healing.

This they did. They prayed earnestly. Fervently. Passionately.

Sandy tried desperately to believe that it would work. She was carried along on the tide of the apparently unswerving faith of those interceding for her.

She was annoyed at herself for ever doubting the point of this spiritual exercise. How could she dare to doubt when all around her were so convinced?

But something kept nagging away in her mind. Chipping away at her confidence.

She had two artificial eyes.

Could their prayers turn artificial eyes into real ones?

Sandy had to have this matter cleared up. So she voiced her concern in the prayer meeting.

"How can anything happen to me?" she enquired. "I have two artificial eyes, you know."

They assured her that the God in whom they all believed was a God of miracles. And He, who had created her in the first place, could cause eyes to form in the waiting sockets. All she had to do was have sufficient faith to believe that such a thing could happen.

The strength of their argument and the depth of their faith convinced Sandy. She left that house that night believing.

Days passed.

Nothing happened.

Weeks passed.

Nothing happened.

Sandy was still hopeful.

She prayed to God. She loved Him, and He loved her. She knew that He would never fail her. He had promised that He wouldn't.

After six weeks Sandy became a little doubtful. Surely something must be wrong.

She went back to the people who had prayed for her, that Friday night, and said, "Nothing has happened."

Their response shocked her that night and shook her faith for months.

"Go home," they replied. "You can't be healed. You haven't enough faith."

When Sandy pondered this statement, in quiet and solitary moments, it distressed her.

Had she let herself down by her lack of faith? She had certainly let herself down before all the pragmatists who had told her that it couldn't happen. How she had argued with them, contending confidently that it would be no problem to an Almighty God to perform a miracle in her life!

And that raised another question. Had her God, whom she trusted implicitly, let her down?

Then, after eighteen months of morale-boosting employment, perhaps the worst thing that could happen, did happen. Sandy's job at Finlay Packaging came to an end.

Now she was unemployed again.

And her faith had been severely dented.

Was she back to square one?

CHAPTER TEN

Going God's Way

❖

Back to square one again, Sandy thought. That's where I am. Hopelessly blind and a recurring failure.

During the ensuing dreary days of unemployment, Rosemary Agnew, a friend of the family, passed on to Sandy some literature about an organisation called The Torch Trust. This group worked mainly amongst blind and partially-sighted people.

The literature was sound and contained some interesting information. Sandy was impressed. One of the leaflets intimated the commencement of a Torch Trust fellowship group in Belfast.

Sandy was invited to attend that inaugural meeting.

She accepted the invitation, and went along.

It was there that she first met the directors of Torch Trust, Mr. and Mrs. Heath, who because of their seniority and overall caring role, had become affectionately known to the members as "Mum and Dad Heath".

During the tea-break, Mrs. Heath remarked to Sandy, "I think we are going to see more of you in the future."

"Hmm," Sandy replied. Suitably non-committal. She had no desire whatsoever to be rude to this kindly sort of a lady, but she thought inwardly, "I wonder what put that idea into your head? You will hardly ever see me again."

Sandy wanted to be treated as a fully integrated blind person in a sighted world.

This was a meeting mainly for blind people. And it had never been her ambition to spend the most of her time meeting mainly blind people

One meeting like this would be enough for her. Thank you.

As time progressed, Sandy's faith began to strengthen again after the shocking shake-up it had received. Christian friends were very kind to her, although she recognised that her continual dependence upon them must often have proved tiresome.

People found their own level in coping with her disability. Many of the folk who helped her through those turbulent days are still among her closest friends.

One of the greatest tonics of her early twenties was to become her involvement with Young Life Campaign and United Beach Missions. Preparing for, and participating in, these organised campaigns, renewed in Sandy a sense of spiritual worth. And belonging.

Her witness proved effective.

When she stood up on the box on a beach somewhere and sang with deep feeling, "I Am the One", "Just a Closer Walk With Thee", or "The Old Rugged Cross", people stopped. And stood. And looked. And listened.

Then Sandy testified to her faith in Christ. And the marvellous change that it had brought to her life.

And still they stood. And looked. And listened.

Sandy soon discovered that she was being used to God's glory. This was gratifying. She was also given opportunities to witness to a variety of age groups and was pleased to find that God enabled her to adapt to any situation.

There was one evening, when she was conducting a coffee bar on Belfast's Shankill Road with Pastor Val English, that a group of young lads came in.

They listened intently as Sandy sang.

Afterwards, while chatting to them over coffee, Val asked, "What did you think of that, lads?"

"It was just like being in the pub, only better", one of the young chaps replied.

Val and Sandy were amused. It wasn't exactly how they would have described their coffee bar effort! But the lads had obviously been impressed.

Though these times were wonderful, and Sandy enjoyed every moment of them, they only served to whet her appetite for greater spiritual things. She wanted to know more and more about her Bible and her God. She yearned to become even more useful for Him.

So to put her desires and her talents into practice Sandy started a meeting for the children of her neighbourhood. It was held in the garage at the side of her own home, on a Tuesday evening. About fifty children attended this meeting regularly every week during the winter months. The kids came from all sorts of homes and backgrounds.

Sandy loved them all.

She sang with them, and to them. She prayed with them, and told them about Jesus and His love. And about how He had called, and was still calling, little children to come to Him.

These Tuesday-in-the-garage sessions proved to be very worthwhile.

The children enjoyed them, the parents appreciated them and the leader felt fulfilled. It was often tiring, but definitely rewarding work.

Still there must be more. Something else, something more permanent that Sandy could be doing for God.

During a missionary conference which had been convened by Young Life Campaign in Portrush, a very simple statement that a missionary made in the course of his talk challenged her heart.

He just said, "Any willing Christian can be used by God."

"That must include me," Sandy reasoned. " I am willing. I really want to be used by God."

She discussed the situation with a leader of Young Life, Michael Barrie.

Mike and his wife had always been encouraging to Sandy and she respected the wisdom of his counsel. He was very positive and recommended a year at Bible College.

Capernwray Hall was suggested.

A few days later, after she had taken a meeting, Sandy was invited back to a home for supper. She shared with the lady of the home, as they chatted together, that she was contemplating a year at Bible College.

Christa, her hostess, asked her, "Have you anywhere in mind?"

"Yes, Capernwray Hall," Sandy replied, quick as a flash.

There was an immediate and unexpected response from Christa. "I was a secretary there for three years," she chuckled. "I will send a letter in along with your application form."

Sandy was delighted. Now she could see that God was leading her gently along, step by step.

One thing, just one single thing, worried her though about going away from home.

It was her children's meeting. Tuesday nights in the garage.

She had established such a good relationship with the boys and girls. What would become of them if she went away? Would she be letting them down, failing them, in some way?

And what about the parents who had trusted her with their children? What would they think?

Sandy wrestled with this one for days. Then she received an assurance from God.

Could the Almighty God, who had saved her and turned her life around so dramatically, not look after a few children for her in Belfast?

Of course He could!

She would go to Bible College.

To Capernwray Hall.

CHAPTER ELEVEN

Capernwray Hall

❖

In April, 1974, Sandy commenced her year in Bible School. Capernwray Hall had accepted her readily, making it clear to her, though, that if she found the course too taxing, she could withdraw at any time.

As she travelled across to Capernwray, on that first day, with a number of other new students from Northern Ireland, Sandy realized during the getting-to-know-you conversation that they were all just as apprehensive, and as excited, as she was.

What was in store for them all? What was it going to be like?

Sandy had two additional concerns. Peculiar to herself.

Number one was to do with the College. Would they be able to cope with all the additional demands of her blindness? And the second was the niggling worry about her own ability to stay the pace. She had been sent home so often, classified as either unwilling or unsuitable, that she wondered if she would ever complete this course.

She certainly wanted to. For God. And for herself.

On arrival at her destination Sandy discovered that the Bible College was housed in a building of rambling design, situated in tastefully landscaped grounds.

As she moved around for the first few days, finding her way about and talking to almost everybody she met, she learnt, too, that there was an international flavour about her new environment. The one hundred and thirty or so students came from many different countries.

It was all so strange to Sandy. But it must have been even more strange to some of the foreign students. For although she was blind, Sandy at least spoke the language!

As study commenced, and a week or two passed, Sandy developed a healthy love and respect for her fellow-students. She was struck by their zeal for God. Many of them had relinquished potentially lucrative positions in their own countries, to prepare for Christian service. She also liked the way they treated her. Just as one of themselves. They were helpful without being patronizing. Caring but not condescending.

The staff, too, were very accommodating, making every possible facility available for her needs.

One of the biggest obstacles that Sandy and her tutors had to surmount was how to deal with the lectures. A blind student couldn't just open a ringbinder, take out a pen, and start to make notes. Sandy's cumbersome Perkins Braille typewriter had to accompany her to every lecture. And of course she needed her Braille Bible as well. All seventy four volumes of it!

After some deliberation the Capernwray management arrived at a simple solution to the problem. They allocated to Sandy, for her own personal use, one of the translation booths normally used by foreign students. This became, in effect, her own little office, accommodating all her paraphernalia.

Although there was much serious study at Bible College there was also a lot of fun. Billy Strachan, who during Sandy's time there became Principal, helped to create this relaxed and informal atmosphere. He used to joke with Sandy about her blindness.

It became a kind of a ritual for him to ask each morning, in front of all the students, before lectures began, "Well, Sandy, what colour are my shoes today?"

His blind student would invariably give him the correct answer. This puzzled Billy for months. How did she do it? It was almost the end of the year before he discovered that Sandy had some of the other students primed to tell her what he was wearing every morning.

It was also Billy who caught Sandy out on the prowl one evening. In those days, lights had to be out in all Capernwray Hall residences at 10 30. Without fail. No question.

The students had other ideas though. They just loved dorm. parties.

There was a very popular soft drinks machine in the hall downstairs. Normal sighted students needed a tell-tale torch to find their way to the machine along the pitch-black corridors. But Sandy didn't. About the only advantage of being blind that she could think of was that the time of day didn't make any difference to her. Day and night were both the same!

So she became the messenger.

One night, just before midnight, when Sandy had finished purchasing an armful of drinks from the machine, and was about to return to her dorm., Billy came along.

"What are you doing down here at this time of night?" he enquired, with pseudo severity.

Cans of drink scattered in all directions.

"Oh Mr. Strachan, it's you!" Sandy exclaimed, startled. She then scuttled off, back to her bedroom, leaving the good man to do what he liked with half-a-dozen dinged tins of Coke and Fanta!

During her year at College, Billy was to prove a great help to Sandy. He went out of his way to try to understand her as a person and to appreciate the additional problems posed by her blindness. The warmth and depth of his Christian concern were a stabilising influence on this keen, but often insecure, student, both emotionally and spiritually.

It was during a chat with him in the dining-room one evening after a meal, that he remarked, "I believe that God is going to use you in full time service for Him, you know, Sandy."

As she moved towards the later stages of her year at Capernwray, she began to feel that God was leading her in the direction of Torch Trust.

Two incidents were particularly significant. Signposts for Sandy.

The first was when she was talking to a group of the other students and telling them how fortunate they were to have so many textbooks that they could use.

Sandy was grumbling, really. Was it not grossly unfair to her that there were so few Christian books in Braille, her language?

This blindness again! Making things hard for her as usual.

After listening to, and understanding Sandy's moans, one of her fellow-students tapped her on the shoulder and asked rather pointedly, "Tell me this, Sandy, what are you doing in communicating the Gospel to blind people? They would listen to you when they wouldn't listen to the likes of us. You have been ideally equipped for a work like that."

There was a poignant pause. The speaker had a point. And he knew it. He must also have sensed from the reaction of the others that they appreciated it, for he went on, "Have you ever heard of Torch Trust for the Blind? I'm sure they could use someone like you."

"Aye, I have heard of them O. K." Sandy muttered in reply.

What she didn't confess to, though, was that she had been to one of their meetings back at home, and her natural pride had whispered, "You don't really want to be mixed up with blind people all your life, do you?"

Had God other ideas, perhaps?

On another occasion the staff of Capernwray had asked Sandy to address all the students, and themselves, on how they should deal with people with disabilities.

She was thrilled to be asked. Here was a chance to make a name for herself! Addressing the entire College on a subject in which she alone had painful, practical experience !

She thought long and hard about it. Prepared thoroughly.

When the day of the talk came around, then, Sandy was really ready.

And she truly went at it! Let them know a thing or two! It was tips on how to cope with disabled bodies and wounded hearts, delivered with genuine feeling by someone who had both.

She gave what she considered to be a wonderful talk. Best in her life, so far. No doubt about it!

Her audience seemed to rate it fairly highly, too.

They thronged around her, afterwards.

"That was great, Sandy!" they enthused........

"That was a marvellous insight you gave us there, Sandy!" they commented......

"Thanks ever so much,Sandy. That was fantastic!" they congratulated..........

It was while walking back to her dormitory from the lecture hall, alone, later in the evening, that Sandy heard God speaking to her.

"You are a real hypocrite, you know, Sandy," He said, in the stillness. "You really excelled yourself there. Telling other people what they should be doing. How they should be treating the blind and handicapped. Why don't you reach out to blind people with the Gospel, YOURSELF."

Sandy struggled with it. Yet again.

"Lord, I am willing to do almost anything for You," she mused. "But please don't let it be amongst blind people. I am now integrated into the sighted world. These people here accept me as an equal. You know that, Lord. And I don't want to end up as a freak amongst freaks. You know that, as well."

It was a promise with a reservation.

A commitment with a condition.

Sandy Clarke was beginning to recognise, though, that God had His quite specific plans for her life . And that His plans were different from her aspirations, in many respects.

When her year at Capernwray Hall came to an end, Sandy realized that it had been vital to her for a number of very important reasons.

She had learnt much. About herself. About God. About the Bible.

She left that College with a tremendous sense of achievement for it was the first time that she had left any school, of any kind, anywhere, with any sort of a certificate.

But there was more.

She had more than a certificate.

She had a certainty.

God wanted her to be His light in blind lives.

CHAPTER TWELVE

Here am I, Send Me

❖

In the summer of 1975 Sandy was back at home and witnessing for Christ in various ways.

As a result of these outreach efforts, three blind people, in three different locations, came to know Christ as Saviour. This was encouraging, but also challenging.

Was God still trying to tell her something?

At this time, also, Sandy was invited to a Torch Trust Fellowship Group weekend in Bangor, N. Ireland.

Again, Mr. and Mrs. Heath were there. Leading, guiding, counselling, and inspiring. During the weekend it was announced that a Torch Trust Fellowship Group was to be set up in Glengormley, where Sandy lived.

"I could help with that," she thought, at once.

Still the urge inside was prodding away at her. About committing herself full-time to the work of the Trust.

But, blind people? To work with them all the time. All day every day. Could she? Possibly?

Sandy was to discover at the weekend, however, that she had been harbouring a false impression of the scope of the Torch Trust.

It was not concerned merely, solely and totally with the blind. Sighted people were involved as well.

A misunderstanding had been smashed to bits and Sandy had taken another baby-step forward. Into the will of God for her life.

If she was to take the giant-step of full-time commitment to the Christian ministry with Torch Trust she would need something more definite though, she felt.

Sandy wanted her own personal secret sign. Her Gideon's fleece.

It came.

During her Bible reading one morning, just prior to the inaugural meeting of the Glengormley Torch Trust group, Sandy was reading in Isaiah chapter six.

As she read down the chapter, her fingers skimming the verses, suddenly she stopped at verse eight. It contained a question from the Lord which demanded her attention. It said :-

"Also I heard the voice of the Lord, saying, Whom shall I send, and who will go for us?"

She hesitated, as she read the answer.

She had been gripped by the question.

But could she make the response her own?....

"Then said I, Here am I; send me."

Was she willing to offer herself to God, to be used for His glory? Wherever He would choose. Despite her reservations.

To go. To be sent.

The inaugural meeting of the Glengormley group was held later in that same month.

At that meeting the aims and work of the Trust were outlined and at the end the chairman, Mr. William Montgomery, made an appeal. He simply asked those who wanted to commit themselves to the work of the Glengormley branch to stand to their feet.

Sandy stood.

Immediately and without hesitation or reservation.

To her it didn't just mean a commitment to the area, though. To the blind in Glengormley.

It was a much wider and deeper dedication than that.

It was to blind and sighted people.

Everywhere.

CHAPTER THIRTEEN

Torch Trust

❖

It was on November 18th, 1975, that Sandy made her first visit to Torch House, near Leicester.

She was pleased with the place. It proved to be a beautiful Victorian mansion, set in extensive grounds. But what about the people? How would she get along with them?

When she entered the house, she was happy to discover that she wasn't going to be disappointed in that respect either. A warm, homely, friendly atmosphere seemed to prevail. Everybody appeared to mix well together. Indeed, it was hard to tell who was blind and who was sighted.

The whole set-up had been called the Torch family.

It struck the latest addition as being rather appropriate.

Sandy hadn't just come to Torch House for a pleasant little holiday, though. She had come to work. To serve the Lord. To be useful for Him. So she was soon introduced to the various aspects of the Trust's activities.

They were engaged in a two-fold ministry, she discovered.

It struck her as being like a person using both arms and hands to minister to the needs of others.

There was the arm of literature, used to supply a steady stream of spiritual food for visually-handicapped people in Braille, giant print and on audio-tape. Sandy was pleasantly surprised to find that this literature was distributed in many countries throughout the world.

The other arm was that of evangelism. The reaching-out-to-others arm. The telling-them-all-about it arm. In this branch of the work blind people were presented with the Gospel message, churches were informed of the work of the Trust, and fellowship groups were established.

Although Sandy appreciated the literature that Torch produced, she realised from the very start that most of her work would be amongst the people.Telling them, whoever they were, whether blind or sighted, about the Saviour who had made such a wonderful change in her life.

For the first week or two after her arrival at Torch House, when she had become conversant with all the aspects of the work, and with the youthful enthusiasm of inexperience, Sandy reckoned that things could be improved. Speeded up at least. It all seemed to be a slow, grinding-along sort of an operation, without a lot of tangible, and certainly no spectacular, results.

She thought, secretly, Here am I. I have come. In fact, I have been sent. Have I not been used by God with Young Life and United Beach Missions? It won't be long until I show this crowd a thing or two about evangelism.

Sandy had many, many lessons to learn. And some of them would turn out to be painful. This was not only going to be her work, but also a training ground. The Trust was certainly going to train her. Knock off a few corners. Make her a vessel, moulded, fired and glazed. Fit for the Master's use.

After a few months in Torch House it was thought that Sandy would make a suitable deputation speaker. Encouraging and monitoring the development of the Trust in Northern Ireland.

So she returned to Glengormley. She was back home. To work from there.

However, despite Sandy's best efforts, things didn't progress as quickly, or as successfully as she would have liked.

There were two reasons for this.

Firstly, she was blind. So she couldn't drive. She was therefore totally dependent upon others to transport her to obscure rural locations, often on chilly winter evenings.

The second reason was nothing to do with Sandy or the work. It was because of the situation in Northern Ireland itself. The province was passing through its most violent years, and travelling around, especially at night when most of her meetings were held, could prove extremely dangerous.

Meanwhile, the work of the Trust in England was expanding and more help was needed there. So, in June 1977 Sandy was recalled to Leicestershire, to Headquarters, to base her activities there. On a permanent basis.

She returned to Torch House, a slightly wiser, slightly more mature young woman. God had taught her a few basic lessons in those eighteen months back at home.

She had learnt that she wasn't the mighty Christian influence that she had imagined herself to be. There was no way that she was going to turn the world upside down, single-handed.

"For you have need of patience....." Lots and lots of loads of it...

That was something else she had discovered.

And there were many more difficult learning experiences up ahead.

Sandy Clarke, who thought she had graduated, with honours, in Spiritual Things, was still only in God's Nursery School.

CHAPTER FOURTEEN

Inner Healing

❖

Back at Headquarters everything went well for a while. But Sandy soon became restless. And unsettled.

She felt that this wasn't what God wanted for her. Or indeed what she wanted for herself either. There were other lessons still to be learnt, though. Perhaps God had His own purpose in Sandy's longer-than-she-had-expected stay at Torch House.

One thing that used to totally exasperate her was how that the blind people there accepted their blindness. Their calm capitulation to the inevitability of their condition used to frustrate her, betimes. Why did they not yell and shout and stamp their feet? Or even just moan and complain? Once. Even only once.

They didn't.

There was something else, too, about Torch House that Sandy found hard to come to terms with. It was the fact that she wasn't being noticed, to the same extent any more.

As she went around taking meetings, when on deputation work in Northern Ireland, Sandy was a blind person in a predominantly sighted community.

So she stood out. Was the centre of attraction. The focal point. Was different.

She was noticed.

Now, in her new working environment, Sandy was a blind person in a predominantly blind community.

So she didn't stand out. She wasn't the centre of attraction. She was just one of the residents. No different from the rest.

She wasn't noticed in the way that she used to be.

Her self-esteem was badly dented.

It was difficult to hide her disappointment and frustration. But she tried hard. Surely nobody noticed. Had she successfully bluffed them all?

The answer, as she was soon to discover was, No. She hadn't.

The most of them, Yes. But them all, No.

One person had noticed that Sandy was having problems.

Blindness-bitterness problems. Deflated-ego problems.

That person was Mrs. Heath, mother-to-them-all.

She started to talk to Sandy at every available opportunity. Befriending her. Counselling and encouraging her.

One day Mrs. Heath invited Sandy into her flat to talk things over, in a friendly caring way. In the course of that conversation the disconsolate and disillusioned Sandy really let fly. She opened wide the flood gates of pent-up resentment, and it all came pouring out. In a torrent.

The underlying theme of the whole outburst was that Sandy was basically sorry for herself and sick of almost everything and everybody else.

It was the blindness-bitterness-bandwagon at full gallop.

Mrs. Heath listened in silence. Only when at last she thought that the torrent had been reduced to a trickle did she offer any reaction.

"Sandy, you need a lot of inner healing, dear," she said, gently.

Obviously the experienced counsellor's diagnosis had been spot on, for her "patient" retorted angrily, "And what would YOU know about it?! You are not BLIND!"

It was patently obvious, too, that the healing process was going to be quite a long drawn out affair.

Mrs. Heath had been dead right.

Sandy did need a lot of inner healing. She was suffering, not only from hostility to her handicap, but also from the emotional scars that remained from earlier wounds in her turbulent life.

And on top of all of that was thrown in, just for good measure, her own self-centred, egotistical, here's-me-and-who's-like-me? attitude!

Mr.and Mrs. Heath realized that Sandy had tremendous potential for God, despite all the problems that she had with her own identity. So they decided to make the spiritual nurturing of this young blind woman their own personal responsibility.

Gradually, Sandy developed a deep respect for this caring couple. Here were people, she recognised, who knew the worst about her yet loved her notwithstanding all.

She enjoyed travelling around the country with them as they went to take meetings, telling of the growth of Torch Trust. Sandy learnt a lot about the work of the Trust on these expeditions, and she also developed from her expert mentors the skill of describing the work with such genuine enthusiasm that audiences were touched.

As she travelled from place to place she continued to mature spiritually, steadily. And as she did, she became aware of two facts.

The first was that God could do wonderful things, without her. The story of the founding of the Torch Trust was remarkable. But she hadn't been involved.

The second was the opposite. There was something that she could do for God. With His help, and under His direction. Talking about a work like this could open some tremendous evangelistic opportunities, she reckoned.

Sandy could become involved with these blind people in a personal way. She could empathize with them. She was where they were. She lived life as they did. She understood the bitterness. The barriers. The ever-present sense of frustration.

There was one important difference between her and many of them, however. She was a Christian. She could tell them about the change that Christ had made, and was still busy making, in her life.

It was an inspiring prospect!

Someone else who helped Sandy greatly in those coming-to-terms-with-the-work-and-herself days was Dr. Mike Townsend, who himself was blind, but had degrees in computer science.

In her earlier, rebellious days she had always resented any blind person who had "conformed", and "made the grade". Here was yet another hurdle of bitterness to be overcome.

Mike helped her over this one. He, and his wife Edith, were great. So patient and understanding.

Sandy didn't feel inferior to Mike. Nor did he set himself up as being in any way superior. He just treated her as an equal. Another child in the family of God.

Lessons were being learnt.

By teaching and by example.

During those many months at Torch House Sandy was enabled to identify her weaknesses. And her sensitivity.

She also discovered, that in spite of all her shortcomings, God had a very specific task for her to perform for Him. And that He alone had the mighty power to help her with it.

That power was going to be mightily needed!

CHAPTER FIFTEEN

From Disability to His Ability

❖

Sandy was still rounding the learning curve.

It was only when she thought that she was off the chicane and out on to the straight that she discovered that there were further bends up ahead. The brakes were going to have to be applied again!

She had learnt a lot, but she still had a long way to go.

After a while she began to regard Mrs. Heath, her patient friend and spiritual guide, as being in some ways an obstacle to her.

In trying to counsel Sandy she would often say, "Give God your disability, Sandy. Let Him use it as He pleases, for His glory."

This often-offered advice infuriated the one it was supposed to help.

"How could I give God my disability?" she fumed inwardly. "And even I could give it to Him this minute what would He do with it? Has He not got problems enough of His own without taking on my disability?"

Away deep down in the depths of her emotions Sandy still resented her handicap. Inner cleansing, though diagnosed and prescribed, hadn't taken place.

She still hated her disability. Not only did she have the blindness to cope with, but she became acutely aware, again, of her lack of brain to hand co-ordination. Her all-fingers-and-thumbs-ness.

Blindness on its own was bad enough.

But had she not been dealt a double dose of disability?

Despite fluctuating spells of feeling sorry for herself, there was one thing that never changed. Sandy loved her Lord. Coupled with that steadfast love for her Saviour came a genuine respect for the well-intentioned Mrs. Heath.

She had a real desire to please them both.

So she promised, albeit rather half-heartedly, "Lord, I will try. That's all I can say. For Your sake I will try to cope with these handicaps."

But how would she do it?

All the other blind residents of Torch House seemed to have skills of some sort.

Some of them were very gifted at craft activities.

Sandy wasn't.

Some of them could type quickly and so were very useful in the literature production and distribution work.

Sandy couldn't.

Some of them, too, had done well at school and had academic qualifications.

Sandy hadn't.

One evening the rumbling, smouldering volcano erupted again.

It had been one of those days in Sandy's life when absolutely nothing had gone right. She felt depressed. Defeated.

Mrs. Heath was sitting, writing, at the end of a table when the door opened.

Sandy burst in and then burst out, "The scrap-heap, that's all I'm good for!

Go on, send me home! I'm no good to you! I'm no good to anybody! In fact I'm good for NOTHING!"

Raising her head from her work for the first time, Mrs. Heath said softly, "Come over here a minute, Sandy."

After a very brief hesitation Sandy crossed the room. As she approached the table Mrs. Heath reached out and took her hand.

Then she continued gently, "I just wish that I could talk and sing about Jesus the way you do."

Having paused for a few seconds to allow that thought to sink in she went on again, tenderly urging, "Give it to Him, Sandy. Give Him your disability. It is crippling you. God wants to use you greatly. Make yourself available to Him."

On previous occasions Sandy had thought, "Here we go again. There must be a crack in the record. Same old thing. Over, and over, and over, and........"

But not this time.

She was a broken woman now.

And she wanted so much to be "available to Him."

Suddenly her heart filled with pain and a lump came in her throat.

"Lord, take away my pride," she blurted out, standing there, one hand resting lightly on the table, the other still held by Mrs. Heath. "Take away my foolishness. It's You I'm following. Not myself. I want to be used by You....."

As she prayed that prayer in all humility, Sandy had a revelation.

It was a tremendous consolation to her. And it was something that had never even crossed her mind before. It was one aspect where she had "one-up on" sighted Christians.

Like a bolt from the blue it struck her.....

The first face that she would ever see would be the face of Jesus!

What a thought!

What a prospect!

It was then that she prayed with heartfelt sincerity and in deep reality, "God, please take my disability, and turn it into Your ability."

CHAPTER SIXTEEN

The Priest Hill Story

❖

Having committed herself, with all her problems and all her talents, to God for His use, Sandy became much happier. And much busier.

Her occasional trips back to Northern Ireland brought her much pleasure. It was great to be with her parents again and to meet all her Christian friends. As news of the work of Torch Trust spread she was also receiving more invitations to address church meetings.

One of those friends who Sandy never failed to visit on her home-for-a-while trips was Margaret McGarry. The two young women had met while working with a Young Life team during a summer outreach campaign.

Sandy became a regular visitor in the Mc Garry home. Everyone in the family made her very welcome and treated her as one of themselves. It was great.

The family recognised, however, that Sandy was more than just Margaret's friend. They saw in her someone whom God had used. And could use.

It was Margaret's father who arranged one of Sandy's first meetings in her home province to tell of the work of the Trust.

A simple invitation from Margaret, a few months later, to speak at a Youth Club was to prove a double blessing to Sandy.

This club was held every Friday evening in Priest Hill Methodist Church, near Hillsborough in Co. Down.

Sandy liked the whole set-up from that very first evening. There was a good crowd of lively, enthusiastic teenagers present. As she mingled amongst them, chatting to them, Sandy was whisked back in thought to the instability of her earlier years. Many of these young people weren't church-going-types but she could identify very genuinely with them. And with the problems of growing up.

When she rose to speak and sing to them then they listened intently.

Sandy was impressed with these frank young teenagers. They must have been impressed with her too, for they asked Margaret to bring her back again!

So Sandy went back. And back. And back....

She enjoyed being in the company of these no-airs-and-graces youngsters and their dedicated leaders. As time passed she got to know Michael and Patricia Mc Carthy and Peter and Victoria McCready who helped Margaret with the club. She felt so relaxed amongst them. She could just be herself.

It was a great thrill to Sandy when the leaders told her, in May 1977, that the Priest Hill Youth Club members were organising a sponsored walk to raise funds for Torch Trust. She felt honoured, and humbled, both at the same time.

Sandy attended that sponsored walk to encourage the young walkers, and to thank them for their efforts. It was wonderful for her to be with so many sincere people, who had sacrificed other interests to raise funds for the work which was so close to her heart.

An even greater thrill was in store for Sandy, though.

In July of that same year, when she was back in Torch House, she received a letter from her friend Margaret.

In the letter Margaret explained that the leaders and members of the Priest Hill Youth Club had been thinking for some time about adopting a full-time Christian worker to support. Having considered Sandy's close involvement with them, and obvious interest in them, they had unanimously decided that she should be that person. They undertook to support her where they could, practically, and to follow all her activities with prayerful interest.

Sandy felt even more honoured, and even more humbled. Both at the same time.

The people of Priest Hill were to prove as good as their word. They conscientiously fulfilled their pledge to Sandy over the coming months and years.

For her part, Sandy was pleased to visit them each time she returned to Northern Ireland, updating them about her work with Torch Trust, and presenting the claims of Christ to the young people. Challenging them to live for Him.

After a few years Margaret married Ken Patterson. It was a husband-and-wife team who now helped to organise the Youth Club, and who kept in constant touch with their "missionary."

Sandy was very grateful for this support as she continued to mature in the service of the Lord. Now that she had committed herself unreservedly to God, He was gradually leading her along, step by step, teaching her a number of basic lessons about His ability to provide for her every need.

It gave her great joy, too, to see a number of these teenage fellows and girls turn to the Saviour, develop in their faith, and eventually become leaders in the group.

She also had confirmed to her, through her involvement with these people, many of whom had no formal church connections, something which she thought that she already knew. Namely, that there was still a lot to commend about the young people of her generation.

A powerful potential for good. And for God.

CHAPTER SEVENTEEN

'Singing for My Lord'

❖

One of the aspects of life at Torch House that Sandy really enjoyed was the music. They had formed their own choir, initially for pleasure and relaxation.

The young woman from Belfast hadn't been long in her new home until she heard about the choir. And she hadn't heard about it long until she decided to join.

Now here was something that Sandy could throw herself into with great gusto. Music and singing were two of her main interests in life.

She was about to experience something of a culture shock, however.

Her style of music was somewhat different from that of the choir, she discovered!

Sandy's early musical educators had been the radio and the record-player. The Fiesta Ballroom and cafe juke-boxes. All rock and pop. Swing and beat.

Now here she was, landed with a group of respectable Christian people, singing traditional Christian hymns. Not that there was anything at all wrong with the hymns. It was just that she didn't know many of them. They had never been part of her life-style.

Yet another phase of schooling and adjustment loomed up ahead. How would it all work out?

Jill Ferraby trained the choir. Jill had always considered herself more of a classical type musician, but she had the experience to recognise in this new recruit a talent and enthusiasm that the choir could well do with. So she trained Sandy too.

The two women spent many practice sessions together. They went over pieces again and again, perfecting the production of Sandy's voice.

Soon Christian groups in the area began to hear about the Torch Choir. The word spread. They found themselves being asked to sing at women's meetings, church functions and in the local prison.

On an ever increasing number of occasions they found themselves travelling to more distant locations to address Torch Fellowship Groups.

This ministry in song became more popular. And it also began to grow and expand. Jill was constantly on the look-out for new items to introduce into the choir's repertoire, to add a bit of variety to the programme and to maintain the audience-interest.

One of these innovations was Sandy. Singing solos.

These solos-by-Sandy progressed from being, as they were at the start, a popular part of the choir's programme, to becoming a vital part of it. Essential. Expected-by-audiences.

As years passed the choir became involved in longer periods of outreach activity. Staying away. Conducting short missions.

Sandy was very pleased when their first tour of Northern Ireland was arranged in 1985, and proved to be a great success. Those who sang and those who listened both considered themselves blessed. The Torch Choir sang and told of their work to attentive audiences who in turn confessed to being challenged by the message, whether spoken or sung.

Following a number of very rewarding tours, the Torch Family Singers were forced to re-examine the extent of their ministry. Things were changing.

Some of the original choir members moved on to fulfil commitments elsewhere. Then there had also been a rapid and encouraging growth in the literature ministry. This meant that the choir could not be available for long campaigns.

They were needed back at Torch House to help with the increasing workload.

Sandy, however, felt that she should continue in the outreach ministry. This was something to which she believed she had been called , and for which she had been equipped, by God. Mrs. Heath had recognised this years previously, and Jill had helped her develop it with her patient voice training.

So after some careful and prayerful consideration, Sandy established her own team musical ministry, to complement that of the choir.

Two lads, both accomplished musicians, joined her, in 1986, to form a trio.

David, who was blind, was a gifted pianist.

Trevor, who was partially sighted, played the guitar.

Together the three of them, after some time spent in practice, developed their own unique style of country and western gospel music.

It wasn't long until they, like the choir before them, began to be in demand. They received invitations to take services in a variety of churches and groups across the country.

The Torch musical outreach was now able to perform a dual role. The choir still sang at a limited number of functions within easy reach of Torch House.

Sandy and the two young men, ably advised by Jill on matters pertaining to music, were able to undertake a more wide-ranging type of ministry.

God began to bless their efforts in evangelism.

Hearts were touched. Souls were saved. Lives were restored.

Sandy felt fulfilled, at last.

Mrs. Heath had been right all along.

God could take her disability and turn it into His ability.

And He was prepared to prove it, too, given half a chance.

CHAPTER EIGHTEEN

'Something Worth Living For'

❖

After Sandy had come to the point where she was willing to dedicate herself and her disability to God for His use, invitations to speak at various types of meeting began to come in steadily.

One of the greatest challenges of her ministry came in September, 1987. Sandy was conducting a mission with a Torch Fellowship Group in a town in the south of England when she was invited to speak at the Sunday morning service in the local prison. That Sunday was to be their last day of mission, and what a climax it proved to be!

It was still early in the month, and hot, as Sandy and her sighted escort approached the prison gates that morning. She had no lads with her this time. No back-up. All she had was her omnichord and her total dependence upon God. He had planned this for a purpose, she was convinced, and so she was equally convinced that He wouldn't let her down.

On being admitted to the prison they were welcomed by the chaplain.

His initial greeting was not altogether encouraging. "Well, Miss Clarke," he began, "you will have thirty-five minutes. But if you are wise you will only take five."

"I am in your hands," Sandy replied. "I will do whatever you think is best. How many will we have?"

Sandy could sense that there was no smile on this man's face as he replied, dryly, "Twenty if you are lucky. It's more likely to be only half-a-dozen."

As the chaplain left to make further arrangements in relation to the service, Sandy and her friend waited expectantly. When the chapel doors opened it wasn't half-a-dozen prisoners that burst in, rowdily. Or even twenty. There were more than one hundred of them! It would be an hour out of their cells on a hot morning, when there wasn't an awful lot else to do anyway.

However, these men hadn't just come to enjoy a quiet Sunday morning's worship. At least half of them, it seemed, were spoiling for a fight. They were only there for the aggro. Insults flew. Then chairs. Mayhem ensued. Extra officers were called to the chapel. The would-be-speaker and her escort sat spell-bound. Sandy prayed, "Lord, please help me to last five minutes here, never mind thirty-five.!"

The service began. After the chaplain had mumbled his way through a few prayers, he introduced Sandy.

As she stood up nervously, all the guys whistled and stamped their feet. She offered an instant prayer for help. "Lord, what do I do here?" was her simple, silent request.

The answer was as instant, and as simple, as the prayer. "Do nothing," came the definite leading. "Just sing."

So without any further preamble Sandy took a few steps forward and began to sing, shakily:-

"Life was shattered, hope was gone,
Crushing the load that I bore,
When out of the depths, I cried, "O God,
Give me something worth living for....."

Sandy's voice steadied as her confidence returned. The volume increased as she began the chorus:-

"Something more than my yesterdays,
More than I had before,
Something more than wealth or fame,
He gave me something worth living for."

Before the song was finished a hush had descended on the room. The chairs and the insults had ceased to fly. There was a peculiar, uneasy silence. It seemed that the prisoners had been quietened by a mysterious influence outside of themselves.

Immediately upon finishing the song Sandy commenced to speak. She didn't want to waste a minute in case the fight was billed to go another round...

"Lads, let me tell you how Jesus gave me something worth living for," she said.

And she then continued to speak for the full thirty-five minutes, having been given respectful attention.

At the close of the service the men all queued up to shake the speaker's hand.

Suddenly one big fellow surprised everybody by stepping forward and requesting openly, in front of all his mates, "Miss, take me to Jesus. Take me to Jesus."

Others showed a fleeting interest, took booklets, and returned, grumbling, to their cells.This chap persisted. He refused to budge. Standing there resolutely he just kept repeating, "Take me to Jesus. Take me to Jesus."

Sandy realised that she was dealing with a genuinely seeking soul. This was no mere passing fancy. He really meant it. "I can't take you to Jesus," she counselled gently, "you will have to go to Him yourself. But I can tell you from the Bible how to trust in Him. And I can pray with you."

That was exactly what she did, too, when afforded the opportunity.

A prison officer, the chaplain, and Sandy accompanied the young man into a small side room. Sandy prayed with him, and for him. As soon as she had finished, the lad began. He poured out his life story before God in sincere confession. His life, and his body, were in a mess. He was in the last stages of heroin addiction, and was convinced that he was going to die.

He cried desperately, "Jesus, I can't fight any more. I am coming to You with all my sin. Please forgive me, and take me. Take me now."......

After accepting the Saviour so gladly, that new Christian stepped out of the small private room and addressed the others who were hanging around, thinking that he had "gone soft". "Fellows, I want to tell you that I have given my life to Christ," he witnessed courageously, a tear glinting on his cheek.

By that time the lad wasn't the only one in tears. Sandy was sitting just in behind the door, weeping tears of joy.

She left that prison that day with a light heart. What an encouragement! How God had used His Word, and her testimony, to the blessing of this earnest young man.

Recognising that her responsibility to this new believer didn't end with his conversion, Sandy arranged for a local Christian to go into the prison and hold a weekly Bible study with him.

Eighteen months after that memorable Sunday, and after the chap had been transferred to another prison, Sandy received a letter informing her that he had passed away. Before his death, however, he had led four of his fellow-prisoners to Christ, and they, in turn, were witnessing in their respective prisons. Pointing yet more to the Saviour.

She was so glad, as she wept over that letter, that she hadn't walked out of that rowdy prison chapel on that hot September morning, as she had been so tempted to do. Sitting quietly, reflecting on the young prisoner's conversion, the second verse of the song which had been so used, came into her mind. Sandy sang it softly to herself:-

"There with life at its lowest ebb,
Who could heal and restore?
Jesus came and He mended my broken heart,
And gave me something worth living for."

CHAPTER NINETEEN

A Very Special Ministry

❖

It was marvellous when God blessed in the work, and everything seemed to be on the up and up. Sadly though, there were other times in Sandy's life and ministry when nothing significant seemed to be happening. And her service for God was being attacked. Both from without, and from within. She spent days, even weeks sometimes, in the doldrums. Becalmed. Travelling about from place to place but going nowhere for God. It seemed to be all routine work. Run-of-the-mill, more-of-the-same kind of stuff. And what was worst of all, very few people appeared to appreciate her efforts, however well-prepared or well-presented.

Following a meeting in a prison in 1989, Sandy shared her concerns with the chaplain who had invited her there, and who was a dedicated Christian.

"Sometimes I think that I am not really getting anywhere with my ministry," she confided in him. "I feel as though I am going round in circles, if you know what I mean. I am doing all this travelling about and putting a lot of effort in with precious little to show for it. Even the Christians aren't the easiest to work with many a time. There are times when I reckon that I am not much use. That I'm not cut out for the ups and downs of this work. For there seem to be far more downs than ups. There have been one or two occasions recently when I have felt like packing the whole thing in, and maybe trying something else........"

Perceiving that Sandy was being attacked and discouraged by Satan, as he himself and so many other full-time workers for God had been from Bible times until that very day, he decided to talk her through it.

"What exactly is this ministry of yours that you talk about, Sandy?" he enquired, as an opener. "What does it include? And who is it geared towards? Is it to old people, young people, blind people, sighted people, disabled people....? Who? What is really in question?"

Sandy thought for a minute or two before attempting to give any sort of a reply. She could sense that her chaplain friend was genuinely concerned about her, and interested in her work, but she had never been asked to define it so specifically before.

"I don't honestly know," she responded at length, adding wryly, "but there is one thing I do know. It is not always easy!"

The chaplain sat silently. Listening. Waiting.

Aware that he was waiting to hear some further explanation of the nature of the service in which she was engaged, Sandy continued, "My work. You want to know about my work.... Well, I suppose it is not something that I sat down at my typewriter one day and wrote out an action plan for... God just seems to open the doors and I go through them... Ten years ago I would never have dreamed that I would become so involved in prison work, for example. Yet, in recent years, I have witnessed in some of the most secure prisons in this country. I still maintain that when God took my disability, He transformed it into His ability. And that ability has opened many doors.."

As she was constrained to think about, and then describe, her ministry, Sandy began to realise that perhaps things weren't so bad after all. Her disability. Becoming God's ability. It wasn't everybody who could talk like that. The chaplain could sense that her self-confidence was returning, but he wanted to draw her out even further.

"And when you take a meeting, in a Torch Fellowship Group, or a church, or somewhere like that, what is it that you actually DO? I know what your style has been in prison, for I have heard you a few times and it has been great. Are your other meetings more or less the same? A blend of speaking, praying, singing and telling your testimony...?"

"Yes, basically they are," Sandy answered, warming to the subject. "I depend very much upon the Lord for guidance. If I feel a word from the Lord is needed, then I give it. If there is an opportunity to sing, I take it. And I love to pray. I have adopted this approach in all sorts of denominations but it has never caused any offence. It is difficult to put what I do and where I do it , into cosy little compartments. "Little boxes all the same." The scope of my work defies precise definition. But there is one thing that I have learnt, and proved over and over again, and that is unless I put the Saviour at the centre of every meeting it will be a waste of time. So I have made that my singular aim. To exalt the Lord Jesus. And I have discovered that when He is "lifted up" He will draw all kinds of people to Him, as He promised He would."

When Sandy had finished, said her bit, run out of steam, she awaited her friend's response. He was in no hurry, however. He knew that this chance to voice her concerns had helped Sandy. And he also recognised that there was something unique about the work that this blind woman had been called upon to do by God.

His reaction to all the explanation, and his summing up of the situation, when they came, were a tremendous boost to Sandy. He avoided the temptation to embark upon some theological treatise. It wasn't the time for that.

Leaning forward, he just said simply, and with a smile, "Ach Sandy, yours is a very special ministry."

CHAPTER TWENTY

Richard

❖

Back to the family. By this time in Sandy's life her sister Marlene, of whom she had been so jealous in her teenage years, was married and had two sons, Richard and Steven.

Aunt Sandy was very proud of both boys. Steven, the younger boy was quiet and rather shy. Richard, the older, however, was different. He was full of fun and mischief. His aunt and he seemed to hit it off well together for Sandy recognised a number of her own natural tendencies being displayed in her young nephew, though she still loved both boys equally.

It was Sunday, 11th June 1990, Marlene's birthday. Sandy was speaking in various churches in Eastbourne, Sussex, on that day. All the old jealousies had long since been forgotten, so she was somewhat annoyed with herself that in all the hustle and bustle of her daily routine she had forgotten to send her sister a birthday card. In order to make amends, at least in some degree for her omission, she decided while walking along the pier on a relaxing, Sunday afternoon, between-services stroll to phone Marlene from a call-box. Wish her "Happy Birthday".

There was no reply. Strange. But it was a lovely summer afternoon. Perhaps they were out somewhere. So she phoned her mum. There was no reply there either. This was very strange. Her parents were always at home on a Sunday afternoon. She had contacted them then hundreds of times.

Sandy began to feel uneasy. An eerie sense of foreboding crept over her. There was something wrong. She just knew it. But what?

On phoning another relative, Sandy found out that her sister, and her parents, had all gone to the hospital to visit someone. But who?

By that time two things had happened. Panic had set in, and her loose change had all run done. Her companions obtained more change for her, and she phoned an aunt. Sandy didn't need a telephone directory. She carries masses of numbers in her head!

At last, somebody who could let her know what exactly was going on! Her uncle told her that there had been a road accident on the previous Friday evening and that Richard, who was almost eleven years old, had been seriously injured.

When Sandy returned to the house where she was staying, her brother had been trying to contact her. She phoned him back.

Things were very serious indeed. Ronald was able to give the whole story. Richard's life was in the balance. He was on a ventilator. The prognosis was not good.

Anxious weeks followed in which Sandy and many other Christians throughout Britain prayed earnestly for Richard's recovery. Although she was committed to fulfilling her pre-arranged programme of meetings, Sandy kept abreast of developments by phoning home every day. She was planning to return to Northern Ireland in early August.

At the end of July, Richard's condition was still giving cause for concern. No-one could be quite sure of what permanent damage had been done in the accident.

Sandy phoned an aunt one night to hear the latest update on his condition. "Sandy," she began, tearfully, "he can't see. And it doesn't look very hopeful, either."

Considering the extent of his injuries, Richard did make a remarkable recovery. God answered the many, many prayers for

Richard and the medical staff were most attentive. All his faculties returned, except one. His sight. Richard's optic nerve had been damaged. He was blind. At age eleven.

Sandy's immediate reaction, when she heard that her young nephew's blindness had been confirmed, was one of horror. "Oh God, please. Not again. Why? Why? ..."

She felt for her parents. How were they going to take this? A double dose.

And Richard himself. How would he take it? How would he adapt? Physically. Mentally. Emotionally.

As time progressed after the accident, and days became years, Richard's capacity to cope with his disability surprised everybody. Now his aunt Sandy is forced to confess often, "You know, Richard is a better Braillist than me, and I have been at it all my life!"

There is still much healing going on in the family since Richard's accident. Though always well-intentioned Sandy has occasionally been indiscreet in her timing when passing on the comment which proved to be such a challenge to her, "God can take your disability and turn it into His ability."

Through her contact with Richard, in his present condition, Sandy has had reinforced for her, a lesson which she should have already learnt. That is that the Lord has His own way of working in people's lives. And His methods vary vastly from individual to individual. Her answer isn't necessarily Richard's.

Sandy now tries to encourage her nephew in every way that she possibly can. To grow up into a young man in his own right. To establish his own identity. To make his own way in the world.

And he is succeeding remarkably well at it!

CHAPTER TWENTY-ONE

'When you Stand Praying, Forgive'

---- ❖ ----

The ministry was going well in the early nineties. God was blessing. Souls were being saved, and Christians refreshed. Sandy felt
really happy and fulfilled. "Oh Lord, this is the mountain-top", she
often thought.

The trouble with the mountain-top, though, as so many have
found, is that if you make any move at all, the only direction you can
possibly go is down.

This proved to be Sandy's experience. Early in 1993 she
became aware that a small cloud was forming on the horizon of her
life. As the year advanced it began to grow and darken, threatening
to create a storm that would block out the sun completely.

It all stemmed from her past life. Sandy had made some big
mistakes. She had said and done some things that were rather
imprudent. She knew that. What she also knew was that these
indiscretions had been brought humbly and tearfully to God, and
had been forgiven by Him.

Unfortunately, others who had heard of these matters were
unaware of Sandy's soul-searching before God. Some people
appeared to have short memories and unforgiving spirits. They

began to cast up the past. Stories of incidents in her past life were being gossiped about, embellished for effect and subsequently misconstrued.

Sandy knew that she was in the Lord's hands and that He would vindicate her in His own good time. But the waiting was hard.

And worse was still to come.

Some of her fellow-workers at Torch House couldn't understand why she felt free to continue with her work for the Trust , "with all these rumours flying around".

This was hard to take. Criticism from non Christians she had come to expect. Criticism from misinformed Christians in distant locations she had learnt to cope with. Shrugged it off with the comment, "They obviously don't know the whole story".

This was different. These were the people she worked with day after day. She loved them so much in the Lord. They were "all one in Christ". Sandy realised that she hadn't always been wise in how she had handled things. She had been awkward, obstinate and downright stupid many a time. But then again, who hadn't? Surely they had all made mistakes from time to time. She had thought that her co-workers would help her, console her, talk things through with her. At least protect her.

That didn't happen. Instead, hurtful and in some instances generally untrue, stories were being spread around.

Sandy became increasingly bitter. Her ministry began to suffer. She was lapsing into feeling-sorry-for-herselfness again. She had started to blame her stupidity, her fellow-workers, and in her most embittered moments, even her God, for the mental and spiritual mess she was in.

What was she to do?

Now that she had become discouraged in her work, Satan attacked again. He kept saying, "You might as well pack the whole thing in this time. You are no good. You know that and now everybody else knows too. Stop. Quit. Give it up."

It came to the point where Sandy found it difficult to continue. How could she go out every day and work with these people, knowing what they had said, or were saying, about her? Could she ever forgive them? And how could she ever forget?

One evening Sandy arrived home after a meeting at which she had found it very hard to speak. Her mind was in a whirl.

She started to have her quiet time of prayer and Bible reading, but she just couldn't concentrate. In frustration she cast herself down at her bedside and cried out to God from her heart, "Lord, if only you would sort this business out for me. And sort these people out!"

There in the stillness Sandy heard the Lord say to her, "I think I had better start with you. Sort you out first. Are you willing to forgive "these people", who you want Me to deal with?"

"But Lord, I can't forgive them. How could I? Look at the things that are being said about me that aren't even true!"she retorted, almost angrily.

The Lord is slow to anger. "I love them just as much as I love you," He continued patiently with His obstinate child. "I died for them too, you know. You MUST forgive."

Deeply convicted in spirit, Sandy rose from her knees, and then sat down in her bedroom armchair to commence her Scripture reading. Her portion for the day was Mark chapter 11 vs. 20-26. She began to read, her bulky Braille Gospel of Mark propped up on her knee.

Her trained fingers skimmed effortlessly across the Braille characters as she read down the passage. When she came to verse 25 she slowed down. Then stopped. Then read it again. She was arrested by the words :—

"And when ye stand praying, forgive, if ye have ought against any : that your Father also which is in heaven may forgive you your trespasses."

Slowly, she read on. And if she had been arrested by the words of verse 25, she found herself condemned, sentenced and punished all at once, by the words of verse 26 :—

"But if ye do not forgive, neither will your Father which is in heaven forgive your trespasses."

Sandy Clarke was pierced through the heart. For three hours that night she remained on her knees, wrestling with God. Begging

His forgiveness for many things, not least of which was her own unforgiving attitude.

At three o'clock in the morning a lightness came into her spirit. She became aware of a real sense of the presence of God in her room. And in her soul. She was forgiven. She knew it.

After breakfast, later on that same morning, Sandy had a telephone call from someone who said, "I have heard and believed stories about you Sandy, which I have now come to realize are not true at all. Will you please forgive me?"

"Yes. Don't worry. Of course I will," Sandy was able to reply, sincerely and without hesitation.

And the work could go forward in power. Again.

CHAPTER TWENTY-TWO

Do You not have a Blind Dog?

❖

One of the questions that Sandy is most often asked as she travels about the country is, "Do you not have a blind dog?"

Understanding fully what the well-intentioned questioner has meant to ask, Sandy usually replies with a chuckle, "I'm afraid a blind dog wouldn't be much use to me, really. But more seriously, since I am travelling about for most of the time it would be impossible to train a guide dog to fit in with my schedule."

The question illustrates the fact that able-bodied people react in different ways to the disabled. The way in which sighted people respond to the needs of the blind, for example, can be interesting. It can occasionally be embarrassing, and is often amusing.

The first group of people are the well-they-aren't-much-different-really crowd.

This category comprises those, who, in an effort to make the blind feel normal and wanted, do not make sufficient allowances for their handicap.

Once, when Sandy was staying with a friend, her hostess suggested that they go to feed the ducks on the pond in the park just round the corner, after dinner. So they set off, suitably armed with a bagful of mouldy bread.

When the lady had Sandy positioned at the pondside she fumbled in the bag of bread. The ducks, ever on the lookout for their next meal, quacked across.

After waiting for a few minutes until the ducks had arrived in sufficient numbers, the hostess shouted encouragingly, "Throw, Sandy! Throw now!"

Sandy threw. As hard as she could. And hit her kind duck-feeding friend smack up the side of the face with three slices of gooey, mushy loaf !

Well, she couldn't see where she was throwing, could she?

Another time, at the end of a meeting, Sandy asked, as she often does when time permits, "Does anyone have a question?"

A rather pompous lady had one, almost at once. "I would like to ask," she began confidently, "do you drive the car?"

Sandy stood there, speechless. She so much wanted to laugh, but knew she daren't. Good manners forbade it.

In the silence of amused disbelief that followed, the lady's companion said, in a stage whisper, "Don't be so daft! She can't SEE!"

Unaffected, and obviously unconvinced, the questioner retorted, "But these blind people are so wonderful! They can do such clever things, you know!"

When she had regained her composure, Sandy said, with mock seriousness, "If you fancy taking a short-cut to heaven just lend met the keys of your car and I will drive you home! Then we will both be in the glory together!"

The direct opposites to the treat-them-very-much-as-normal group are the over-compensators. These are the people who, because they are unsure of themselves, or have not had any experience in dealing with disability, are inclined to treat people with a physical handicap as being mentally retarded.

For some reason this trait often becomes evident in the tea-and-chat session after a meeting.

Once a tea-lady addressed Sandy's escort and whispered, "Would she like a cup of tea?"

Whereupon the escort, not quite sure whether to be embarrassed or just plain angry, replied, "She is of age, ask her. Surely she is old enough now to speak for herself !"

At another meeting in an inner city location two little old ladies were sitting behind Sandy as she helped herself to her tea and buns. One half-shouted to her companion who must have been half-deaf, "Edna, did you ever see the like of that blind girl? She is just after lifting her cup, taking a sip of tea out of it, and setting it back right in the middle of her saucer! Isn't that marvellous?!"

Sometimes Sandy takes visiting church groups around Torch House. The building is old and many of the floorboards squeak.

As she was guiding a ladies' group through the house one day, Sandy heard one of her charges whisper to a friend, "Aren't the floorboards very squeaky?"

Her friend, who knew about these things, whispered back, "Shsssh, Maisie dear, shsssh ! That is so the blind people will know where they are going!"

It can be awkward at bedtime, now and again.

Once when Sandy had moved into a new area to stay over for a few nights, her hostess showed her to her room, and by moving around with her guest allowed her to become familiar with the layout. Then she just stood there. And stood, and stood, and stood.

Thinking that perhaps there was something else that she needed to know, Sandy enquired, "I'm sure I know where everything is now. Is there something else you want to show me?"

"Oh no, my dear, there's nothing else," her hostess replied. "I am just waiting to undress you and put you into bed."

Trying hard to disguise her surprise at the kind lady's naivety, Sandy said matter-of -factly, "Don't worry, it will be O.K. I should be able to manage perfectly well from here, thank you."

Since people react in different ways to the needs of the disabled, Sandy considers it an essential part of her ministry to help educate her audiences, wherever possible, on the problems that disabled, and particularly blind people experience. And how able-bodied people can best help them to cope.

One of her favourite approaches, when addressing school or youth groups, is to ask her audience to describe a rainbow.

"Oh, that's easy, miss," the students invariably begin. "It is like a semi-circle and it is red and orange and yellow and green and...."

Sandy interrupts them there.

"Don't go so fast," she says. "What is red?"

There usually follows an incredulous silence, which some kind soul breaks by replying, in a condescending tone, "Why, it's a colour".

"And what is colour?" Sandy continues.

That stumps them.

Then it gradually begins to sink in. Here is someone who has no understanding of colour. Has never seen the blue of the sky, the green of the grass or the autumn extravaganza.

Having highlighted the differences between blind and sighted people, Sandy then usually goes on to stake their claim to be treated in the same way, as far as possible. She emphasises to her audiences that they should treat people like her, not as disabled people, but as ordinary people with their own distinctive needs and personalities, who just happen to be disabled.

She also considers it necessary always to stress that everybody, whatever their physical condition, is the same in another vital respect. Each and every person is a sinner who is loved by God, and someone for whom Christ died.

It is important to get that message across, as well.

CHAPTER TWENTY-THREE

Into the Big Time

❖

The greatest love of Sandy's life is her Lord. There is no doubt about that. She loves Him because He first loved her, and when she trusted in Him her life was completely transformed. Following, as a close second to that supreme love, comes her love of singing. It plays such a vital part in her ministry. However, since she is unable to read normal print, and relatively few Gospel pieces have been transcribed into Braille, she is compelled to learn most of her songs by listening.

When considering a new piece, with a view to learning it for herself, Sandy listens to the words and commits them to her very acute memory, but she is also influenced, either consciously or otherwise, by the style of the singer. Since she has developed a style that suits her own particular type of presentation Sandy isn't tempted to copy very many of them.

There have been one or two notable exceptions to that over the years, though.

One such exception was the music of the Gospel singer, Rev. William Mc Crea.

From the first time she ever heard him sing, Sandy was intrigued by his style. And she wanted to try and model hers on it. But it didn't end there. For such a fan had she become that not only did she want to mirror the man's style, but she wanted to meet the man himself. She was sorry that she had never been able to realize this ambition since their paths had never crossed.

One evening after a meeting she was out for supper with some friends. Background music was provided by Rev. Mc Crea, singing to them through a couple of speakers.

"I love to hear that man singing," Sandy happened to remark to her hosts. "He is so sincere. I would really like to meet him some time."

"Would you, honestly?"one of her friends replied. "We could easily arrange that for you. No problem."

Sandy was delighted and John and Eunice Wright proved as good as their word. One afternoon they took her to visit Rev. William Mc Crea and his family at their home.

"I hear you sing a bit. Is that right?" William asked.

"Yes. That's right," Sandy replied. "I must confess I do try to sing a bit."

"That's great," her host encouraged. "Come on then, give us a song."

Unusually for Sandy, she was somewhat taken aback. Here she was in the presence of the person whose singing she had admired for years, and he was asking her to sing for him!

"I—I—I don't have any instrument with me," she stammered. It was only a kind of a half-hearted excuse. She was thrilled to be asked.

"Oh never worry about that," William went on. "Tell me what you want to sing and I will play it for you on the piano."

So Sandy sang, "Something Worth Living For", and he played.

That afternoon saw the commencement of a friendship for Sandy with Rev. Mc Crea and his family. This friendship led to her visiting them on other occasions and to her being invited to sing in their church.

What a joy and privilege it was then, in 1995, to be invited, with others, to take part in the making of the video, "Going Home."

It was a marvellous day. Many Gospel singers, whose singing Sandy had enjoyed for many years, were gathered. And the pleasing thing was that she was accepted as one of them. As an equal.

When it came her turn to do her solo part Sandy was extremely nervous. For not only did she have to overcome her awe of the big occasion, but she had other problems as well. Physical problems. Simple things like getting to stand in the right place. And even just holding the mike.

When it was all over Sandy felt rather deflated. She didn't think she had performed to the best of her ability. She reckoned that she messed things up a bit.

Let herself and her friends down. There was a sickening sense of anti-climax.

"Ah well," she consoled herself as she lay awake that night, reliving the events of the day, minute by minute, song by song, note by note, "they can always edit it and cut out my part if they want to."

Having convinced herself that she hadn't made the most of her big break, Sandy was surprised to receive a phone call, a few days later, from someone in the recording company which had organised the video.

"You did well the other night, Sandy," he assured her. At least that was comforting. But she had no idea what was coming next!

"How would you feel about recording a cassette and C D of your own?" he proposed.

Sandy was flabbergasted.

She was so sure that they would have to cut her out of the video. Now they were suggesting that she do a tape on her own! She had recorded a few tapes before back at Torch House. But these had not been distributed widely in Christian bookshops. This would be different.

When she had given her consent, a date was arranged, and Sandy recorded the album, "He Washed My Eyes", in June 1995.

To Sandy's great delight her tape was released on the same evening as the video, "Going Home".

Both the video and Sandy's cassette have proved to be a blessing to many. There is still never a week goes past but somebody writes in, or phones up, or just approaches Sandy after a meeting somewhere to tell her how that God has really moved, or comforted, or challenged them through the music.

Her disability yielded to God.

And His ability displayed.

It was, and is, still true. For her, at least.

CHAPTER TWENTY-FOUR

Travelling On

❖

Sandy Clarke has travelled thousands of miles in deputation work for Torch Trust over the past twenty-two years and she has often been moved to tears by particular experiences.

One such memorable event was her visit to Malawi in 1994. Torch Trust have established a work amongst the blind people of that African country and Sandy had the pleasure of representing them as part of a team on a visit there.

Her singing proved popular with the Africans. So too did her testimony. People flocked to hear about what God had done in her life, then talked about it for weeks afterwards.

The impact of the visit wasn't all one-sided, however. Malawi left a lasting impression on Sandy. She was convicted by the positive attitude of the many blind folk. They didn't have any Jordanstown School for the Blind. There were no Social Services. Very few training-centres. Most blind people, including the believers, had to beg for a living. It was their only chance of survival.

Sandy recalled the first twenty years of her life. How she had complained bitterly. And rebelled furiously. Yet she never once had to beg for anything!

The visually-impaired Christians she met on her travels in Malawi just seemed to have a singular aim in life. That was to learn more about God, and His love, and His Word. And to praise Him, and praise Him, and praise Him.

That visit was a moving highlight of her ministry. A real privilege. A life-affecting experience.

Most of her travels, though, have been across the length and breadth of the British Isles. And over the past two years a fair percentage of her travel has been to new venues to conduct meetings arranged after an initial contact has been provided by the video or the cassette tape.

Wee Mrs. Thingmajig from Ballymacholy will ring up and ask, "We would like to know if that blind woman, Sandy Clarke, takes meetings? Could she come on Tuesday evening / Saturday afternoon / Sunday morning and speak at our Youth Group / P.W.A. meeting / D.C.F outing / Fellowship hour.... ? We saw her on the video "Going Home"."

This increase in bookings has led to an increased burden being placed upon those volunteers who so gladly arrange Sandy's itineraries.

For twelve years Myrtle Stone handled all of the bookings that came in. Myrtle performed this task very efficiently until she had to relinquish her responsibility owing to other commitments.

So great has the demand for Sandy's ministry now become in Northern Ireland that it has been necessary to create a base in her home Province to administer her busy schedule. A Torch Trust office has been set up at the home of Cecil and Irene Bingham, near Ballyclare. This kind couple have arranged her travel for a number of years, but they haven't merely been transport managers. In many, many cases they have provided the vehicle and been the driver, helper and porter. On arriving at a venue this versatile pair immediately double up as stage managers and sound production team!

Sandy spends the first three months of each year based in Ireland, travelling to conduct meetings in both the North and the Republic. Cecil and Irene have taken her to many locations, both large and small, in big cities, in small towns, and in remote rural communities.

For the remainder of the year she travels all over Great Britain, sometimes with her backing group, "the lads", as she calls them, sometimes with Eileen Cole, her friend and escort, but often alone, singing and speaking. Simply proclaiming the wonderful news of the Gospel.

Wherever she goes, and regardless of who is with her, it is a thrill to witness the manner in which God blesses the message, whether in word or song.

Nevertheless, Sandy knows that she cannot ever afford to become complacent. She is conscious of the fact that although many new opportunities have presented themselves, there are still hundreds of blind people in Britain who have never heard of the Saviour and His love.

It is them that Sandy wants to reach.

They are her mission field.

She is often asked, as she travels around, "How is it that you get to speak at so many meetings? Do you send out and ask people if you can come?"

The answer to that one is always the same. And it is always simple. "I never ask anyone to have me," she explains. "I just leave it to the Lord. He goes before me , and opens up the way."

Like all of us, Sandy doesn't know what the immediate future holds for her. Where she will be called upon to go, and for how long she will be spared to continue, she leaves entirely to her Heavenly Father.

All she wants to do is what she has learnt from often-bitter experience to be her best, indeed her only sensible, option.

It is to make herself availabe to Him for use, where, or when, or how He chooses. He will do the rest.

One thing she can say, and sing, though, with absolute assurance and genuine depth of feeling, and often does, is....

"Oh, the joy of sins forgiven,
Nothing's the same as before,
My life overflows, since Jesus came,
And gave me something worth living for."